THE

PLAYBOOK

*7 Fundamentals of Financial Planning,
Organized and Addressed*

Benjamin James, CFA, CFP

Content in this material is for general information only and not intended to provide specific advice or recommendations for any individual.

This information in not intended to be a substitute for specific individualized tax or legal advice. I suggest that you discuss your specific situation with a qualified tax or legal advisor.

DEDICATION

This book is dedicated to an inspiring lady whose
'beacon of light' will be shining for a very long time.
In memory of Linda Paxton, thank you for being so strong.

Methods are many. Principles are few.
Methods always change. Principles never do.

—*Proverb*

"As to methods there may be a million and then some,
but principles are few. The man who grasps principles can
successfully select his own methods. The man who tries
methods, ignoring principles, is sure to have trouble."

—*Harrington Emerson*

CONTENTS

APPENDIX 1

How to Build Your Own Playbook

The Playbook is a tangible object you get to hold onto, walk around with, share with your advisors and pass on to someone when it's time to turn over the business of running the household finances to someone else.

Here is a simple set of instructions on building your actual playbook.

Step 1: Create the Folder

a. I Recommend a three-ring binder with a three-inch spine.

Notes:

A three-inch binder is easy to store. This might seem a small measure to keep all of your financial affairs in. However, following the methods described here, with the focus on keeping only what is important, you will develop a Playbook that's not only easy to use but easy to tote around with you. *My busier than most financial life fits quite nicely into my Playbook.*

Also, you might consider using a bright and easily recognizable color. In our office as we prepare these for clients, we use a bright blue color that can easily be picked out amongst personal items. Our clients have expressed the satisfaction in knowing when something happens to them, their Playbook is easily located by people who need to have it.

b. Create eight different sections by using dividers and label each section.

  a. Goals and Objectives

  b. Financial Statements

  c. Estate and Legal Documents

  d. Insurance

  e. Taxes

  f. Performance

  g. Social Security and Pensions

  h. Miscellaneous

Notes:

Make your dividers durable and easy to jump from one section to another. You might consider large labels to easily identify where a section starts.

In addition, you might consider purchasing 'sheet protectors' for your Playbook. This can help as you are replacing old statements for more recent ones. Not having to open the three rings of the binder is a nice step to avoid not to mention avoiding having to hole punch everything you need to keep.

You should be able to cover all of your financial affairs in these suggested sections but hey, this is your Playbook. You get to customize and design one that is perfect for you.

Step 2: Start Filling It up

a. Use your Playbook as part of your mail sorting so you can get acclimated to the process.

b. Start to go through your existing files and move them to the Playbook to clean up your old habits.

c. Methodically work your way through each section using this book as a reference tool so you cover all aspects of your financial household thoughtfully.

Notes:

You may find that you are now using your shredder more often and recycling more than you have in the past. That's great, it means you are not hanging onto useless information.

At this point, make an effort to wean yourself from going to the filing cabinet to store stuff. <u>It is all going to fit in your Playbook</u>, that's the idea. In fact, as you start to use the Playbook, you will be eliminating many if not all of those files you might already have going.

As you reduce your files, take the time to notice what you have saved in the past and give yourself time to understand what it is that actually needs to be saved in the future. Ask yourself questions like, "Why did I save this in the first place?", "How old is this?" and recognize when you saved something and never needed it for anything.

<u>*Reduce clutter and focus on what is important!*</u>

Step 3: Maintain It and Share It

a. Once you've completed the sections of your Playbook, update it periodically.

b. Share your Playbook with people who might need to make decisions for you. At the very least they should know where to find it.

c. Bring your Playbook to your financial appointments. It holds the answers to your various advisors' questions.

Notes:

A good practice is to update your financial statements each year or every time there is a significant change. Ordinarily, I'll update my Playbook each January, so I'm dealing with all the new statements at once. However, if I buy or sell a piece of property, pay off a loan, open or close an account then I might want to update my Net Worth Statement and records right away.

Once you've gone through the process of getting your I's dotted and T's crossed and your Playbook is complete, it's time to share it with your spouse, kids, or whomever you trust. While talking about money is personal for many of us, the business of running your financial household deserves a continuity plan. <u>Someone needs to take the reins when something happens to you.</u> If you want things to run efficiently, giving them the occasional reminder of how the system works is a great idea.

Foreword by Dr. Rick Jensen

Author, performance coach, sport psychologist

When was the last time that you were pitched a quick-fix solution to a problem? In today's "have to have it now" society, there exists an unquenched thirst for the latest fitness gizmo, nutritional supplement, or tech app that promises us success with minimal effort. I only wish this were true!

Having spent my professional career coaching elite performers in both sport and business, I've had a unique opportunity to observe what the best in the world do to achieve success. Many believe that these champions employ secrets that others do not know or cannot access. Certainly, there must be fast-track tactics that those at the top use to separate themselves from the rest of us.

The reality is that there are no quick-fixes, short-cuts, or insider secrets that elite performers rely on for success. The undeniable truth is that champions, across all arenas, follow three defined steps to achievement: 1) understand the fundamentals—what drives results, 2) create a plan to master these fundamentals, and 3) execute the plan.

In *The Playbook*, Ben James applies this time tested process to help you master the area of financial literacy. Like sinking a 10-foot putt in golf or hitting a backhand in tennis, financial literacy is a skill that is developed over time with understanding, planning, and execution. As you read *The Playbook*, you'll quickly realize that you've turned to the right professional. Ben is a champion in the world of financial advice. HIs financial knowledge, thoroughness, and genuine care for his clients is unparalleled.

Whether your net worth is $500 or $5,000,000, Ben's *Playbook* provides you with the road to financial confidence. *The Playbook* outlines the 7 fundamentals of financial literacy. Ben has effectively provided you with everything you wanted to know about your household finances but didn't know what to ask. *The Playbook* delivers simple, practical explanations of the financial factors that are or will be impacting your household—taxes, insurance, social security, estate planning, just to name a few. You will learn what to track, who to speak with, what documents to keep, and for how long. Finally, you will get answers to the myriad of financial questions that you've pondered over the years. After reading *The Playbook*, you will have increased confidence that you understand your family finances and are tracking them successfully.

If you are like many, you have financial and legal documents scattered randomly in file drawers, safety deposit boxes, or on a computer. *The Playbook* will help you get organized. You will finally rid yourself of financial and legal clutter by creating a system that puts everything in one place. Ben teaches you how to create your own personalized plan within each of the 7 financial fundamentals. With a plan focused upon what's relevant and essential, you can securely navigate the complexities of the financial world.

Finally, *The Playbook* provides you with a step-by-step system to execute your plan. You will learn from Ben that a plan is only as good as the level upon which it is implemented. In my work with professional athletes, what stands out is their willingness to walk the talk. Once they establish their training plans, champions execute. Ben empowers you to do the same with specific actions you can take within each of the 7 fundamentals. Using *The Playbook*, you will become a champion of your financial household.

Most People Don't Have a Good Financial Plan or an Effective Organization System

It's hard to talk about money for most people and understandably so; it's a social taboo. The wealth each person attains is so different from one person to the next. Feelings of pride, resentment, worry, and envy are all strong feelings—feelings that encompass the topic of money to such a degree that we don't openly talk about our finances.

Talking about money can open the door to your or someone else's anxiety about money, or create envy, or expose pride. Most of us don't want to make other people feel uncomfortable. We also run the risk of finding out we don't have as much as we thought we did. And for many, far too many people, we just don't want to talk about what we don't have. It's no secret just how 'broke' the vast majority of people are in the world.

Talking openly about money in our culture just isn't done in most circles and as a result. I would suggest that culturally we have cast darkness on something that is undeniably important for every household to manage effectively. And this shadow is cast wide. It's related to your investments, money in the bank, home value, taxes, pensions, social security, insurance, and ultimately your estate.

Because the conversation of money often lives in the shadows where we don't disturb it, I think most people have been undereducated about how to take care of their money. That is a real problem for us, and it has contributed to the vast majority of Americans being behind in retirement savings, being unable to accomplish their financial goals, and unsure about how to make what amounts to some fairly easy decisions.

I've always dedicated a significant amount of my time thinking about, managing, growing, and distributing money. However, that doesn't mean that I'm hyper-focused on being rich. In reality, money is just one of those things that we need to have, but for most of us, it doesn't need to be the main focus of our lives. My view of money has evolved over the years to this; it is necessary and useful, but it is just one of many tools available to us. I understand that it isn't 'everything', but I think I can say that it is a pretty important 'thing'.

Where My Money Mindfulness Started

My fascination with money started as a young child when I got my first paper route. In those days, we'd fold the papers, deliver the papers and then once a month collect the funds for the papers. After paying off the area distributor, we kept what was left. It was a great system for a grade-schooler (although the era of ten-year-old delivering papers in the early hours before school is probably over). I suspect that having been exposed to routinely handling money as a child may have contributed to my long-term career in financial management, or at least I like to jokingly say so.

INTRODUCTION

After my early paper route years, I spent time as a busboy, waiter, and a valet. All my jobs seemed to be paying me cash tips in those days. I even remember during junior high and high school spending time ironing my dollar bills. Once I got my bills ironed and often starched—oh man, there is nothing like a freshly starched dollar bill—I'd organize my stacks by denomination and then by serial number. All face-up, of course.

My early fascination with handling money and organizing my cash created the momentum I needed to pursue a degree in finance. It was through my formal education in finance that I learned about how the *'business world'* viewed finances. Somehow, I always knew that ironing your bills was not the definition of taking care of your finances and college opened my eyes to how the professional world of 'money people' think.

As I continued my education, my mind was opened to how clever financial gurus viewed leverage, cash flow, and other things like the time value of money. I was exposed to how accountants manage the big picture of corporations by running balance sheets and income statements; how finance departments viewed liquidity needs, cost of capital, and long-term planning of funds. I'm very grateful for my opportunity to study finance. That education and degree in finance led me to my career as a financial advisor.

As a financial advisor, I pursued and obtained the Certified Financial Planner designation (CFP), the Chartered Financial Consultant (ChFC) designation and became a CFA (Chartered Financial Analyst) Charterholder. The designations I earned complemented my earlier academic preparation in corporate finance. Techniques from both the study of corporate finance as well as personal finance were used to create the Playbook.

Running a household finance plan like a business has some advantages that can't be overlooked. The business class has figured out how to systematize, streamline, and create efficiencies in a disciplined manner that was appealing to my bill-ironing roots. It took some time to marry the concept of personal finance and corporate finance, but when it finally happened, it was magical, and it paved the road for the Playbook.

The Genesis of the Playbook

After decades of practice as a financial planner, I've heard hundreds and likely thousands of personal financial stories. Clients tell me what their issues and challenges are. I hear about the struggles they have as well as their success and triumphs. I also hear about the estate planning strategies developed by attorneys, developed over a family dinner without an attorney and even passed down from generation to generation. I hear about the stuff that shows up in the mail and how confusion exist over what is important and what is just irrelevant. I see the filing systems of households and the impact it has on those who pick up the pieces when something derails that household. I see beneficiaries wade through box after box of meaningless paperwork making sure they don't overlook something that might be important. Mostly though, I see and hear people express frustration because they don't understand how the disciplines of finances overlap and work together and they don't have a meaningful way of interpreting all of the information.

INTRODUCTION

After decades, I have some insight into the pros and cons, pitfalls, and benefits of most financial planning methods. The lack of understanding surrounding household finances is enormous. Out of the multitude of stories I've heard, they all boil down to some very common issues. These issues are not typically complicated or challenging to solve. Yet they often go unresolved and can cause potentially significant problems for some very good people. It's not laziness or a lack of information on the subjects. It's just a discipline that hasn't been learned by most people, and perhaps because of the taboo nature of money, we've done a horrible job as a culture teaching and learning this subject. For this reason, we developed the Playbook.

The Playbook is not allocation advice and will not tell you anything about how to invest your funds. The Playbook does not solve your tax problems, legal problems, or insurance needs. It's not meant to replace the act of managing your investments. These things are either left up to your advisors or left up to your own devices. All of these things will be accomplished if you tackle them though, and you will use your Playbook to store, review, double check, and be mindful of your affairs.

The Playbook *will* help you:

- get rid of clutter
- track your net worth
- document expenses and income
- help you articulate and document your goals
- enhance, manage, and develop estate planning strategies
- serve as a reference book for those that might have to pick up where you left off

- help track and manage insurance
- help prepare for taxes
- help manage social security and pensions (some of your biggest financial decisions)
- gather all of your important information into one cohesive spot that will allow your team of advisors to assist you with accomplishing your goals holistically
- most importantly, the Playbook will give you a system to track everything related to finance so you may address all of the details of your household finances

What's in Your Playbook?

How do you organize and keep track of all the important financially related information for your household? Do you have a system in place that allows you to manage your financial decisions effectively? Do you have your documents in all one place that you can share with your financial professionals for holistic advice? Do you know what to keep, what to disregard, and how often to update your information? Do you have a system that makes sure the I's are dotted and T's are crossed?

The Playbook is a system designed to help us make financial decisions by creating an organization system that lets us focus on what is important and get rid of clutter so we can easily gain a holistic view of our entire financial picture—all in one place.

I hope you enjoy reading about the Playbook, and I hope you get to work on creating your own right away!

CHAPTER ONE

Goals and Objectives

"If it ain't writ, it ain't!"

When I first read the phrase, "If it ain't writ, it ain't," I laughed outloud. Then I repeated it several times in my head and shook it with amazement. It's such a simple statement that you almost intuitively know it conveys an important truth. Applying *this simple truth* to our goals and objectives should lead to a much higher rate of accomplishment and I would tell you from experience I've seen it to be true. <u>Writing down your goals is the first step to accomplishing them.</u> If you write down weight loss goals, business goals and objectives, savings goals, education goals, why would you not write down lifetime financial goals for your household?

Evan though goals and objectives may be different, I tend to use them interchangeably. To me, while a goal is the destination and the objective might be the progress that gets us to that destination, they are both referring to the path we are on. Because they are so entwined with each other, I'll commonly use the phrase goals and objectives to speak about not only the end result but the work to getting to that result.

Documenting Your Goals Reminds You of What Is Important

A long time ago, my wife and I created a family motto: *faith, family, finances, fitness, and fun,* to broadly and boldly represent our family values. We call them the 5 F's. We thought to live our lives guided by the 5 F's and for a while we did, and it was great. The choices we made, our activities we did, all seemed to be very fulfilling because we were making them based on our values.

However, often what happens with grand ideas, happened to us. Life got busy and the day to day operations of living kept us so busy we didn't pay attention to our 5 F's for years. We were just trying to catch up with housework, careers, kids. Life was too busy it seemed. We were making decisions reacting to what was happening around us rather than proactively making decisions based on our values. That's not good. I think back on those years realizing that we'd strayed off course.

When we addressed our 5 F's again, with a little more dedication, I realized how important they were to the happiness that we both experience in life. Why would we not follow these great guidelines that were giving us happiness?

Articulating and documenting our goals is a process that not only can bring people closer together, but it also *reminds us* occasionally that we have this shared vision. That reminder can keep us on track.

In a practical application of documenting your goals, consider the financial decisions made by many that represent a self-control issue. How many people are stuck in the coffee drive through line and can't seem to pay off the credit card debt or get into that first home? We all have self-control issues in one area or another (at least I assume we do because I've never met a perfect person). But, what if as part of a process, oh let's call it writing down your goals and objectives, one was to articulate not being in credit card debt and owning a home. And if that person was to regularly review that goal, would they have a better chance of accomplishing that goal and passing up on the coffee line?

Holding Your Help Accountable and Getting Better Help

When you rely on help for various aspects of your life, you should get *much better help* when you can clearly tell your coaches, trainers, or advisors what you are after.

If my goals are to pass on wealth to my kids for example and pay as little tax as possible, my financial advisor might steer me to an Estate Planning attorney as a result. Or, that might be suggested by my insurance agent, or CPA. I don't know where the advice is going to come from but one of my professionals is likely to know where to turn to help me with my goals. However, if I've not taken the time to write my goals out and share them with my advisors, I might not get that advice. My advisors might assume I've got it addressed already or that my objective might be to spend it all before I pass. Writing our goals down helps reduce the chances that someone else is making the wrong assumptions for us.

You might say that anyone who knows anything should *know* to see an estate planning attorney for a goal like that. Well, you are probably right but… if I haven't even put much thought into articulating my goals I might not consider the tax aspect at all. And, perhaps I go by what *I know* and don't see the need for estate planning or the benefit not realizing how complicated estate tax planning can be.

I could wait for any advisor to simply ask me what my goals were. But, I'd have to wait and honestly my advisors are busy. If they are good, they should ask right? I agree, but how happy are they going to be when you provide them with a written statement of what you want? Very happy I'd suggest.

Finally, when you've shared your goals with your help and advisors, don't you have a much easier time holding them accountable for their advice? That's what we pay them for after all; their advice. If I've clearly articulated my goals, provided it to my advisors and had an open dialogue about those goals, I've now included my advisors on my wishes and objectives. Now they are accountable for how their advice pays off.

Good advisors should be seeking out your goals. Most will appreciate any efforts you have made to give them a leg up on understanding your wants. You not only empower them to be more helpful but you set the tone for making sure they are helping.

Some Things to Address When Writing down Your Goals and Objectives in the Playbook

Now we are going to talk about some topics to address when writing goals for your playbook from the financial perspective, different formats you might use to express your goals and how often you should update your goals.

Additionally, we will dive into the topic of financial projections and discuss the pros and cons of using them in your playbook to forecast your future. But, documenting your goals is certainly not limited to financial goals. Why not add all of your goals to the Playbook? *If they ain't writ afterall, they ain't.*

When you write down your goals for your playbook, what do you say? Creating written goals can be challenging for people I know. It's hard to write down goals when sometimes you don't even know what is possible.

Before I begin, one quick note. My suggestions for what you write down in your playbook comes from a few decades of identifying common goals that relate to the management of someone's financial household. You can come at this from any angle you want, but the important thing is to document. No template of predefined topics will be as meaningful for you as what brings tears of joy to your eyes when you think about it.

Topics to Address from the Playbook Perspective Regarding Finances

- <u>Growth Vs. Income:</u> When it comes to the investments you have or are going to have; do you want them to grow or provide income? Or some combination of the two? If you are years away from a financially independent and work optional lifestyle, then you probably want growth. You should state that. If you are retired, you might state that your objective is income or at least some income and some growth in your portfolio. Documenting this can have the benefit of being able to quickly narrow down your investment selection to those that are relevant.

- <u>Date goal for retirement or work-optional lifestyle:</u> If you haven't crossed that line yet, document your target date here. It can be a range as well (like sometime between age 64 to age 67); you may find that using years instead of ages can be helpful as well (like sometime between 2021–2024). Even if you haven't thought much about the date, the idea of writing it down might help you to start thinking about it more. "If you fail to plan, you plan to fail." as we say. I also find that people who start to pick a number, start to save more and spend less. Funny how articulating our goals can shape our behavior!

- <u>What is your risk appetite?</u> Or rather, how risky are you? If you don't know, you are not alone. Sometimes this is a moving target, but often people will know themselves enough to judge if they are conservative or aggressive or somewhere in-between. There are countless risk tests you can take to narrow it down for you. One of my favorites is Riskalyze.com. While it's a test based around portfolio values, it may also give you or confirm for you a general level or risk in other areas of your life. Within a few minutes you can get a number assigned to you between 1–100. The '1' is the most conservative, and '100' is the most aggressive. Riskaylze can also help you assess your portfolio to give you an indication of how risky it is and assign it a number to see if it matched your risk number. A general rule of thumb is that 100 minus your age should be your approximate risk number and as you approach your work-optional lifestyle, that number should generally be getting lower and lower. The primary advantage of documenting a risk tolerance or appetite is that information should qualify potential investments for you with greater success. Your advisors will surely be able to as well. I also think about the accountability of having documented risk preferences if you are going to work with an advisor.

- <u>How do you like insurance?</u> Would you rather be a little over-insured because you like to have everything covered just in case, or would you rather have the bare minimum of insurance and self-insure on as much as possible. I think about the warranties you can buy on store purchases for things like washer and dryers or computers. I've declined a lot of extended warranties offered and saved a lot of money. However, it could have easily gone the other way; I could be wishing I had that coverage if I had a lot of losses. But the way I'm wired, I'd rather self-insure to the extent I can and save the money. So, my objective might be minimizing the amount of insurance I have to the extent I can because I prefer to self-insure whenever possible. One big advantage of documenting this is not only for conversations with your Help, but also knowing your preferences will help you quickly make decisions when it comes to the type or amount of insurance you are seeking or willing to accept if optional.

- Estate Goals: Do you want to leave as much as possible behind for the kids or charity, or do you want to maximize your spending and let the last check to the undertaker bounce? (Or somewhere in-between?) There is no right answer here. In the years before education and opportunity to the extent we have it today existed, passing down the family farm was a must if the kids were to survive. These days most of us are not farmers, and we provide our kids with educations that allow them to survive away from the farmland. On the other hand, leaving a legacy and creating long-term family wealth is a very powerful thing. Generations and generations of compounding interest can create a tremendous amount of opportunity for those fortunate enough to have previous generations have that mindset.

- Probate Avoidance: Do you want to have your estate avoid probate? If you do, you might consider having your estate reviewed or doing it yourself in some systematic process to make sure the accounts and assets are all set up correctly. There are several tools to consider and when we get into the Estate and Legal Documents section we will cover some of them.

Formats for Documenting
Your Goals and Objectives

Easy Bullet Points

Just the act of writing your goals down might be the most important aspect of this exercise. You don't have to get too creative or detailed, but do get them on paper. The easy bullet point approach is quick and painless and easy to manage.

Start by using bullet points for what you want to accomplish, keep going until you can't think of anything else. Remember, you can always come back to the list and add or delete something at any time. Just get a start and make it happen!

Some examples:

- Retire at 65
- Be debt free in 10 years
- Make sure estate is tidy for kids
- Avoid probate
- Be healthy

The benefit of this approach is that it is, as stated, quick and easy, and it gets the job done. The downside to this approach is that it might be leaving something on the table, possibly specifics, measures, action plan etc.

Current and Future Goals

Another approach is to create a 'current goals and objectives list' and then create a 'future goals and objectives list'.

For example, I might state in my current objectives and goals that I'd like to build wealth to the point where it would sustain my family for the duration of our lives. Or I could say I'd like to save X amount of money. In my future objectives and goals, I might say I'd like to create income from the wealth I've accumulated, or I might say I'd like to withdraw X amount of dollars every year at some point in the future.

The benefit of incorporating future goals is that you are *lending an eye to the future*. Having goals itself is an act of thinking about where you want to be, but creating goals for when you get there is another step in planning. Will your goals change by the time you get there? Yes, most certainly. But not all of them, and the fact that you've been thinking about them while on the path will enable you to deal with refining them and creating new goals much more effectively.

Past, Present, Future

One step forward might mean looking back. I've always loved the saying that *your headlights should be brighter than your taillights*. In other words, focus on the road ahead, not what's behind you.

However, having an eye on what happened can give us some wisdom. Having a record of what our goals once were can show us what we tried to accomplish and what we did. Sometimes just a reminder of what we've done can be enough to propel us forward to do even more.

Having the past goals and objectives incorporated in our work will usually shed some light on our growth and development; it helps us see where we were, where we are, and where we are going. It's a great story.

The Purpose Statement

I like to think of this section as something my kids or grandkids would read, and they would say, "Hey, this is what grandpa and grandma were really about." It helps define and potentially illustrate what our values are and what is meaningful and important to us.

The *Purpose Statement* section might contain statements like:

- We feel it is important to use our assets to encourage the ongoing education efforts around homelessness

- Whatever wealth we accumulate we want to make sure we are doing it in an ethical and non-offensive way to our environment

- Our family value of managing wealth for the next generations should be taught and passed on

- We don't feel it's important to keep up with the neighbors and pride ourselves on living within our means

Or,

- We want to be competitive in our efforts to grow because we realize the importance of positioning ourselves to provide an opportunity for the next generations

- We try not to get caught up in the fad or concerns of the moment and keep an eye out for the long term

- Our inheritance to our children is their education, and we want to foster a sense of education as part of our family culture

- We support the growth of scientific discovery and want our portfolio to reflect this

- We adhere to our strict fundamental beliefs in X and want our lives and financial affairs to reflect this

The idea of adding a purpose statement is to gain some insight and to document your value system. It can serve as an important reminder to yourself as to who you are, and it can provide insights for those with whom you work.

Projections—What Are They Good For?

"Difficult to see. Always in motion is the future"

—Yoda

Projections in the sense of financial planning deal with casting light into the future of your financial health. Or put another way with financial projections, we are trying to guess where we are going to be financially at a later point in time.

You might use projections in a financial plan but please use with a little caution. Sure, it's a nice idea to plot how much wealth you are going to create by sticking to a plan and what better way to plot it out than by creating a wonderful chart or spreadsheet that shows us the money just building and building. It is nice to know what things could look like, but wow, how a reliance on them in the past has created disappointment for people.

Remember the year 2000 when the dot-com market crash occurred? It wasn't just stocks that went south, a lot of things became cheaper because of significant wealth-reduction as a result of the market pull-back. It took nearly seven years to get back to the stock market high of 2000! Then shortly after that, in 2008, we had the financial crisis. It took another 4 or 5 years to recover—just to get back to the levels pre-correction. We had what a lot of people in the financial industry call a 'lost decade.' Indeed, the decade for returns might have been lost, but the investors all got older, and many people didn't realize gains in their portfolios because of the lost decade. That was horrible.

What happened to the projections that were created in 1999? They blew up. How about the ones that were created in 2007? In both of these periods, the projections were way off the mark. One year everything looked on track and the next it appears you were another five years out from your goal. And if you were already retired and had too much risk... you might be back at work!

Imagine plotting the path ahead of you and relying on that map. Meanwhile you are doing all the right things on your side, saving money, adjusting your allocation, and even doing a few sit-ups for good measure. Then you get hit with a huge recession, and your projection is now meaningless or at the very least way off where you want to be.

Your projection indicated you would have X amount of wealth by this date, and now you have 25% less than that. You know you have to hang in there. But you realize that the last time you saw something like this, it took years to regain lost ground. Are you still on track? Well, perhaps not for the destination you originally chose or at least within the time frame you had anticipated.

Projections can be comforting, and they can be devastating. So, why are they important? Well, for one thing, they can show you that if you follow certain guidelines based on historical returns of various instruments or actions and or certain capital market expectations (some of my very favorite confusing technical jargon here), you have a reasonable shot at accomplishing what you want. And, hey, that's a good thing.

Projections are even better at showing us what happens if we don't contribute to our savings.

If you show a projection of assets with no contributions—unless you are lucky to be starting with a large number that is—the projection will certainly show you a fail. Projections may show us the likelihood of something not happening better than the likelihood of actually accomplishing a goal.

For example, you know if you don't diet and exercise (including those sit-ups), you are not likely to meet your weight-loss goals. If you chart out your projected weight loss based on poor diet and exercise habits rather than healthy ones, your projection will show you that you are headed in the wrong direction. You now have feedback that suggests you need to make some changes. That's the great thing about projections—they can tell you when your plans won't work so that you can modify your assumptions or actions. Sometimes, our projections can be better predictors of failure than success.

The point we want to walk away with here is that projections are useful, but they don't predict the future. The future is, after all, "in motion and difficult to see."

How Often Should You Update Goals and Projections?

Your goals and projections should be updated often. I'd suggest a yearly review and update as needed in your Playbook. To achieve your goals, you want to review them frequently. Then at least once a year, you should question them and update them if needed. Let's face it, you can't ignore your goals for a year and then sit down and review them with much expectation of accomplishment. Print your goals, laminate them, and keep them in the shower!

Life certainly changes for us in this fast-paced world in which we live. The annual review of goals is like a mental retreat to sit back and asses where you are and where you are going. It's an opportunity to reflect on what you've learned over the last year that might alter your desired direction.

At one point I had a goal to become a runner. I even ran a marathon. And I learned something about myself doing it. I've got a physical frame that might not be the most suitable for long-distance running. You might say, I'm more of an apple than a carrot. A happy apple! I started having knee problems and back problems—even with great shoes. (Though I'll admit that with good coaching and better advice, I might have continued to run problem-free.) I came to a point where I learned that whatever I was doing, despite my goals, it wasn't working for me. So, I stopped and modified my goals. Now I do Taekwondo with one of my twin boys—and I love it. Periodically looking at our goals gives us a chance to make adjustments.

How the Goals and Objectives Section of the Playbook Ties into the Rest of the Book

- In **the Financial Statements section,** you will see that the Net Worth Statement and Cash Flow Statement should be a reflection of your financial goals. For example, if you write a goal of being a multi-millionaire, you will want to see a reflection of that on your Net Worth Statement from year to year.

- **The Estate and Legal Documents section** covers the documents and what are often the legal 'instruments' that accomplish your goals. If you want your estate to avoid probate, this section is going to probably have a trust or illustrate proper titling of assets to accomplish that goal.

- **The Insurance section** can also be a reflection of your goals. If your goals are to not retain risk yourself but to buy insurance, then you better make sure the insurance section of your playbook is reviewed and matches up with your goals. If you have a goal of providing for your family no matter what, you might have insurance needs.

- **The Tax Preparation section** might show charitable contribution receipts you've collected throughout the year. Or, if your goals are to pay the least amount of taxes possible, it could suggest some aggressive tax strategies.

- **The Social Security and Pension section** might reflect your goal of lifelong income as opposed to cashing that pension account out as a lump-sum. Or you might elect the lump-sum and just live on the earnings if your goals are to pass on wealth. (You don't have a lump-sum option with Social Security Payments but could you imagine if you did?!)

- **The Performance section** – dare I say that performance measurements and goals go hand and hand? Yes, I'd say that having goals leads to the measurement of your progress quite nicely. What do we measure with performance? Hopefully your goals!

Goals: From the Playbook Players

Leaving a nest egg

I once had a client who told me that leaving a nest egg for her only daughter was an important goal for her. Her daughter had a disability, which would impede her ability to maintain a comfortable life if her mom passed away. That became a documented goal and part of our regular conversation. I don't think this mom would have forgotten about this goal even if it wasn't written down. But, because she had expressed her goal in writing, we were able to regularly address whether or not her assets were supporting that goal, and it guided our advice on how to use the resources that she had. We were able to avoid a large selection of opportunities because they just weren't suitable for capital preservation strategies that would support her goal. Further, we were able to quickly make decisions over the years because we had a clear understanding of what we were after. If the conversation starts with the 'why' and when that 'why' is clearly documented, our chances of success are very good.

It was sad to see this client finally pass on, but the daughter is well taken care of now and the mother is well appreciated.

Probate Avoidance

We worked with a couple who documented that they did not want to have assets subject to probate because of the personal experience they had with their parents' assets when they had passed. Additionally, they shared stories they had heard from their friends in similar circumstances that confirmed their desire. This couple felt very strongly that the time delays, cost, and perceived hassles of probate were not something that they wanted to be part of their legacy.

As a result of that written objective, each year, when these clients would review their goals, double-checking registrations became an integral part of making sure that objective was met. Because the clients clearly communicated their goals to their advisors, they received education and up to date information that helped foster an understanding of how to achieve their goal.

When the clients finally passed away, they had three daughters that all received an inheritance free of the hassles of probate. Our office watched as the goals of our former clients were easily accomplished and the daughters benefited from the careful planning of their late parents.

CHAPTER TWO

Financial Statements

Please don't stop reading! Financial statements are not that challenging. You are not going to have to study those prospectuses that come in the mail or read documents filed by large corporations with the Security Exchange Commission; those are not the kind of financial statements that are important to a household. Neither are those alarming, pesky loan documents with high percentage rates and language that talks of penalties and contractual obligations. Nor the annual privacy policy notice or the statement you get from your investment company or the overdraft protection statement you get from your credit union or bank.

All of the forementioned items are probably not worth saving, probably not worth reading, and most likely mailed out to either satisfy a provider's 'policy or procedure' in place or they are mailed out as a matter of regulation and law. Yes, they sound important, and if you can't sleep at night without understanding why you are getting them in the mail, then, by all means, read them, seek enlightenment and understanding—and then declutter and get rid of them. So much useless stuff comes in the mail and I want you to make it stop coming.

To successfully manage our financial house, we need to get rid of the clutter and focus on the things that are meaningful for us.

Two Financial Documents You Want in Your Playbook

There are two financial statements I'll recommend that you prepare— 1) the Net Worth Statement (NWS) or balance sheet and 2) the Cash Flow Statement or budget worksheet. In addition to these two things, you will want to keep your company generated account statements or at least a recent copy for each account. More on all of this later.

How Often Should You Update Your Financial Statements?

Publicly traded corporations need to update their financial statements at least quarterly, but you and I are not a corporation. How often you are going to update your financial statements section of your playbook is a matter of time and preference. When I had the bandwidth or extra time, I would update my NWS monthly. Now I tend to think that is way too often and laugh about even having time to have done that. Most people don't need to know how their big-picture changes on a month to month routine.

My suggestion is this: Update your financial statements at least once a year. If you ever need to present them, they will be recent enough, and it's a great habit to take a look at your finances at least annually. However, if you have a significant change in your finances like taking on a new loan, buying a new asset, gifting significant portions of your assets away, getting a new source of income, or adding a new payment, then you might as well update the financial statements. *At least once a year or anytime you have a major change.*

The Net Worth Statement

The "Financial Statements" section of your playbook begins with the Net Worth Statement. (Oh man, this is going to be fun!) I'll sometimes refer to the Net Worth Statement (NWS) as a balance sheet. Most accountants would use the term balance sheet as well, but for the sake of this book, I'll use the terms NWS and balance sheet synonymously. We will look at an example of a NWS in this chapter.

Think of the NWS as the 50,000-foot view for your finances; by its nature, it takes a snapshot of the big picture. It calculates what you are worth financially in one glimpse. It can also have more granular detail that can be quite important, like ownership and titles. More about that later, but for now, think of the NWS like the bathroom scale. It measures something. (But unlike the bathroom scale, at least for most of us, we want the figures to keep increasing and increasing.)

I realize that, at some point, enough is enough, and I agree with that wholeheartedly. The sake of building more and more wealth to satisfy a hedonistic appetite is just silly in this guy's opinion. Money is just a tool in the tool chest, after all, and who needs to have fifty hammers? In essence, unless you were lucky enough to be a trust fund baby or part of a very elite crowd of aristocrats, you will likely want to build your wealth so it can support you during your years on earth. Potentially, you'll want to leave a legacy or a bequest to loved ones, or you might want to leave something to a cause that is near and dear to your heart.

Why Do We Need a Net Worth Statement, and What Is It Anyway?

When I first got out of college and after passing the appropriate exams (like series 7, 63, etc.), I began to sell investment products. This was *back in the day* when financial advisors were called stockbrokers. Then and still today (although most in the business call themselves financial advisors, wealth managers, or financial planners now) to give financial advice to anyone, we have to do something we call suitability. One important step in suitability is documenting an investor's net worth, among other things. *Net worth is simply all of one's assets, minus all of one's liabilities.*

To me, the terms asset and liability are quite familiar. But I can appreciate that some might struggle with those terms, although they can be easily understood.

An **asset** is simply something of value, like a house. Assuming that you own the asset, it should go on your balance sheet. A **liability** is simply something that you owe to someone else, like a mortgage on a house.

Your net worth can be as simple as the value of the house less the value of the mortgage. So, if you have a house worth $400k and you owe $300k on your mortgage, you have a net worth of $100k—assuming you had no other assets or liabilities. It's quite simple and would look like this:

Net Worth Statement	All Assets minus All Liabilities	Net Worth = 100k
Assets Column	Liabilities Column (Debt)	
Home Value 400k	Mortgage Balance 300k	
Total Assets = 400k	Total Liabilities = 300k	

A goal for many people is to increase their net worth. If you have a net worth in the millions, you are generally considered to be in pretty good shape financially. It is all about the 'net' part of net worth. Simply having a lot of different assets worth a lot of money and yet still owing a large amount of money might look like you've got your stuff together, but it could be a very unhealthy NWS.

Take, for example, the couple that drives that $150,000 sports SUV, lives in the million-dollar house, and has a vacation home at the beach worth $500,000; we might assume these people are millionaires. Of course, we know that isn't always the case. They might owe $140,000 on the car, be upside down on the house owing $1,100,000, and the beach house turns out to be leased and not owned. Based on this example, this couple would have a net worth of -$90k (add the house value of 1,000k and the car value of 150k = 1,150k subtract value amount owed 1,100k and 140k). See the table below. Yes, it is easy, basic math. Not the kind of thing a rocket scientist is going to do at the office. Yet, it's really important to do, even for the rocket scientist. It's important to understand and manage a net worth statement.

Net Worth Statement	All Assets minus All Liabilities	Net Worth = -90k
Assets Column	Liabilities Column (Debt)	
House Value 1,000k	Mortgage Balance 1,100k	
Car Value 150k	Car Loan 140k	
Total Assets = 1,150k	Total Liabilities = 1,240k	

Early in my career, I would calculate net worth quickly but accurately. It's a simple matter, after all. At some point, without being taught, I realized the benefit of documenting the net worth formally and keeping a record of it in client files. The obvious benefits were being able to go back to the records for details and to keep a history of the records so we could track progress. I've always been pretty good at creating spreadsheets, and creating a net worth statement in excel or other programs is quite simple. Yet, back in the day, I was lured into a 'fancy' Net Worth Statement (NWS) Spreadsheet that I bought off of eBay!

I thought my eBay spreadsheet was pretty cool stuff at the time because it had macros that would allow me to create a new NWS while retaining the old data. I could have one NWS for today, one for last month, the previous year, and so on; this created a nice record of my net worth over time and illustrated the record in graph. Funny how that technology of graphing, creating a picture out of a spreadsheet, was so 'state of the art' back then in the late '90s.

Now we have apps and programs that can do so much more. New technology makes my graphing spreadsheet of yesteryear look so very dated. Yet, the NWS, in all of its simplicity, is still the same. While I don't use or look at the graph part of my 'fancy' NWS anymore and haven't for many years, I do still use the same spreadsheet for my NWS that I did 20 plus years ago. Some basic and important things don't change. Calculating net worth is one of those timeless things that fundamentally doesn't change: net worth = total assets minus total liabilities.

How Do We Build the Net Worth Statement?

Here are a few considerations:

- Break the NWS into sections
  - Short Term Assets
  - Long Term Assets
  - Real Estate
  - Personal Assets
  - Short Term Debt
  - Long Term Debt
- Add details like:
  - How the account is registered (individually owned, jointly owned)
  - Include interest rates, especially on the liabilities side
- Be complete and accurate
  - Don't leave anything out—no stone unturned
  - Be realistic on subjective values

Short-Term Asset Section of the NWS

First, let's tackle the short-term asset section; this is usually the first section in the NWS. Here we are going to list every liquid, short-term account that we have. Examples would be any bank or savings account or any short-term CD (less than one year). Or, if you happen to be one of those people who keeps significant 'cash on hand', list it here as well.

What we are not going to list in this section are longer-term assets like retirement accounts or brokerage accounts that hold securities (financial investments) like stocks or bonds. Those will go in the long-term section. Also, we are not going to list things like personal assets where you have a value in mind but finding that right buyer could take months and months. Those items will likely be in the personal or long-term section if considered an investment (think collector car or art).

In the short-term asset section, we want to add some specific detail. When you own an account at a bank, for example, it will have a specific registration.

- If you own it by yourself, then it is an individual registration; this means that it's only in your name, and you are the only one that has access to the funds.

- You might own it with someone else; this is a joint registration. Joint registrations can be tricky as there are typically two types of joint registrations that exist. First is Joint Tenants (JTTEN). This registration implies that while you own it together, if one of the parties dies, then his or her share would go to his or her estate. That can get messy. For example, if one partner dies then the remaining partner might end up owning an asset with people she does not even know or worse she knows but does not like.

- The other common registration type is the Joint Tenants with Rights of Survivorship (JTWROS). This registration implies that you own it together, but if one party dies, then his or her share goes to the surviving party on the account. I might hold a JTWROS with my wife, but I might hold a JTTEN with my business partner.

- You might have instructions on the account that ask the financial institution to transfer or pay the assets to someone else if you die—kind of like a beneficiary designation. Did you know you can add these to almost all types of accounts? Add a Transfer on Death (TOD) designation to brokerage accounts and even real estate. Add a Payable on Death (POD) designation at your bank or credit union. The big advantage here is that these 'little add-ons' like POD and TOD will allow the account to avoid probate. Most people want that for their heirs.

- A few variations of the above mentioned are 'JTWROS with TOD.' Or 'JTWROS with POD' instructions. This would imply that while either one of the joint owners is alive, the assets will belong to them but if both owners die then the assets go to the named beneficiaries.

Once you have the registration type included, you might consider adding an interest rate. In this day and age of low rates, it's easy to assume that these liquid accounts don't pay anything. Well, they typically do, just not very much. It hasn't always been that way, and it probably won't always be that way. The idea of documenting the rate helps us get some perspective on the NWS. If, for example, we've got $100,000 sitting in an account that generates .5%, we might consider paying off debt that charges 10%!

The section of the short-term asset section of the NWS might look like this:

Short Term Assets	
PNW C.U. Jack and Diane JTWROS - TOD	$1500.00
The U.S.A. Bank Jack – individually, POD	$1500.00
Cash on hand	$500.00
JPMorgan CD 2% - J&D - JTWROS - TOD	<u>$15,500.00</u>
Total Short Term Assets	**$19,000.00**

Often, we are trying to fit a lot of detail into a small space. Abbreviations are key here. Notice above; I put J&D to indicate Jack and Diane on one line. Also, I didn't bother to indicate who the TOD or POD recipients (who gets the asset if J&D die—the beneficiaries) are. We deal with that detail in the estate planning and legal document section on our beneficiary review form. However, you could make a note here if you like. Keep in mind one thing though, at some point someone else might have to read your NWS, and if we get too cute with abbreviations, we run the risk of confusing a potential reader. While the NWS is fairly personal, we have to account for the fact of death or the possibilities that someone will have to make decisions for us at some point.

Long-Term Asset Section of the NWS

Welcome to the place on your NWS that we keep track of your retirement accounts! The land of the long-term invested asset, the serving platter of the main course, where your assets have the most potential for growth. While the short-term assets are the liquid reserves that you draw from and sacrifice any real return (at least if you consider keeping up with inflation) in order to presume to be safe—the long-term asset section is where you can afford to take the calculated risk that may very well enable you to achieve much higher rates of return on your invested dollars.

More often than not, your retirement accounts (the IRA, ROTH IRA, 401k, 403b, 401a, 451, and so on) are the perfect place to invest long-term assets. While theoretically you could have a very conservative retirement account and have invested in short-term investments, most investors will take a much longer-term outlook than a single year in their retirement accounts.

Side note: just because you are drawing off of an account or taking income from an account, it can still have a time horizon of decades. Take the recent retiree that draws from an IRA but plans to continue to do so for 20 plus years. Endowments often have current income requirements but are perpetual—the funds are meant to be around infinitely!

You should also put non-retirement accounts that have a longer-term investment objective in this section. If you have a brokerage account with stocks or bonds, include it here. As you probably already know, the big difference between a non-retirement account and a retirement account comes down to tax deferral.

As with the short-term section, don't forget about those registrations. Label the account, indicating who and how they own it. For example, your label might read, 'Jack and Jane JTWROS – TOD stock account' or 'Jack's E-trade Stock account – TOD.' If you have a bond portfolio or an individual bond that pays a fixed interest rate, you might also note the interest rate. If you hold stock certificates (for example, those you might keep in the bank vault or personal safe), you can list them here as well. However, please consider getting those stock certificates into a brokerage account. You will find managing the asset a lot easier that way.

Don't forget about your stock options, warrants, and ESOPs (Employee Stock Ownership Programs). While having a current valuation from warrants and stock options can be a little tricky, we can often get market data on public-traded options that you can use as a close proxy (or substitute) for non-traded options. In other words, if you don't get a published value, don't ignore the asset—just find a close proxy. The important thing to do is list them on the NWS. Leave no stone unturned!

Employee Stock Option Programs (ESOPs) will typically have annual statements, and, at the very least, will indicate value. It can be extremely important to keep track of not only the values but the exit strategy. Concentrated stock positions, publicly traded or not, can offer a tremendous upside to your net worth. But, having a wife who worked for an Enron-owned company, clients who worked in the lumber industry before the real estate crash of 2008, I'm certainly aware of the risk of concentrated stock positions. Always consider how much of your presumed wealth is tied up in one company or one sector of the economy and always know your exit strategies.

Business Owners

OK, if you are a business owner—this is where you are going to put the value of your business. Speaking with business owners for years, I've noticed that they often have a hard time assigning a value to their business's. And sometimes a tendency to assign no value at all.

I've got a friend who owns a septic tank cleaning business. I'll ask him what he carries the business at on his NWS and he'll say to me, "Ben, no one wants to buy this S%$Ty business, why would I carry it on my NWS?" That always cracks me up… After some discussion, he always agrees that the business has assets. It's got various trucks, excavators, hoses and specialized equipment, client lists and more. Not to mention the business checking account (alternatively, the business checking account could be held in the short-term section of the NWS, especially if just one person owns the business). If he were to liquidate all of the equipment and vehicles for the business, he'd have a tidy sum of money. After even further discussion, he might admit that someone would be willing to buy his customer list and assume the name of the business because he's got repeat business coming in.

How you determine the value of your business is important. It can be a very subjective number. In dealing with business owners most of my working career, I'd say that many tend to underestimate the value of their business until they sell, and then they tend to overestimate the value of the business when they want to sell. This book isn't going to dive into business valuation methodology (that's far too deep for our purpose). There are business professionals who specialize in valuations you can hire at the appropriate times. The advice I've always given is to pick an industry standard and stick with the same standard each time you update your valuation until you get a professional opinion. For example, you might have 2x the sales or 4x the net revenue. The multiple may vary from one business type to another but can be found pretty easy.

Regardless of your method, having one that closely represents the actual value will not only help provide a realistic number but it will provide some consistency in your period to period reporting of your net worth. Because a business can be such a large part of the net worth for many entrepreneurs and sole proprietors, it's important to give enough consideration of the value to create a realistic net worth statement.

Pensions

What about pensions? Those who are lucky enough to have a pension certainly consider it an asset but are they really? We should view a pension with care. If the pension ceases to exist once the owner is deceased—it might be more of a cash flow item than an asset. In other words, it doesn't belong on the Net Worth Statement it belongs on the Cash Flow Statement. But, if you don't go to the trouble of creating a Cash Flow Statement (to be discussed later) it wouldn't hurt to put the pension down on the Net Worth Statement so you at least make a recording of it for others to address if need be. The questions might be what value do you put down?

Sometimes pensions will have a lump-sum distribution value. In other words, how much money you could walk away with today while forgoing the pension payments. That value would certainly go on the NWS. But, if you don't have the option of a lump-sum, should you still put a value down? (This is subjective, but I'd tend to say yes.) You might use an approach like a discounted present value of cash flow based on your life expectancy. Finance people like that kind of stuff—if you feel clueless about that task, find a finance person to give you a value. If it's truly just a cash flow item though that disappears at the death of one or two spouses it probably belongs exclusively on the Cash Flow Statement.

Here is a list of other things that might go in the long-term asset section:

- Retirement accounts
- Cash-value life insurance (just the cash value)
- Precious metals
- Stocks
- Bonds
- Options, warrants, ESOPs
- Business interest
- Loans (including family loans)
- Contracts or deposits

Here is a list of things that shouldn't go on the long-term asset section:

- Things already listed in the short-term asset section
- Term life insurance
- Cars
- Personal items
- Real estate
- Anything that you lease or rent but do not own

Once you've listed out all of your long-term assets, they may look like this:

Long Term Assets	
ROTH IRA – Jack	$11,500.00
401k – Diane	$150,500.00
Gold Bars	$500.00
Loan to Jack's brother	$15,500.00
Total Long Term Assets	**$178,000.00**

What about the Real Estate Section?

This section is pretty self-explanatory, right? Well, yes and no.

For many people, the *Real Estate* section contains their house.

Remember though, you have to own the house for it to be on your Net Worth Statement. If you rent or lease, you don't own it.

Homeownership in the U.S. is somewhere in the middle of the sixtieth percentile or rather more than 6 out of 10 people. Most people will own a home at some point. When they do, it's in the Real Estate section. When putting down the value of the home, put down the amount that the house is worth (or rather for what you could sell it). Ignore the fact that you might have a mortgage on the house—we will deal with that on the liability side of the NWS.

Getting a full appraisal for your house every time you update your Net Worth Statement would probably be a big waste of money! Use Zillow or one of the many other online versions of home value assessments. If you like, use three and choose the mid-point between them. If you are not happy with the value or know it's way off then you probably know enough about the value of your house to make your own determination.

Vacation homes also go here, as well. Same as above, if you own the home it's on your balance sheet. If you lease it every year you don't own it.

What about a timeshare? If it is actually yours to sell and has a value it could bring *or* if it transfers to your beneficiaries if something happens to you, you would want to put it on your NWS. Even if you don't feel like it has value and might be more of a liability than an asset, one potential benefit of listing it on the Net Worth Statement is that you are making a record of ownership.

Rental properties are commonplace among established households. Your rental property or properties should be listed in this section. Whether it's commercial property, residential, multitenant, storefront, or campgrounds—if you own it, put it on the NWS.

You might ask the question, "What's the difference between this and the long-term asset section above?" You are right, they are similar, but real estate has some unique properties that you might want to separate from other long-term assets. Liquidity is often an issue. You can't typically cash out of property overnight. Because real estate is often concentrated, it presents a special risk—think about a lot of eggs in one basket. Having all the real estate listed in one place on the balance sheet gives us a nice glimpse at how much we have concentrated in one asset class.

Like the other sections, when you own real estate, you can own it jointly, individually, JTWROS, JTTEN. You can own it in a trust, or you can also attach a T.O.D. (transfer on death designation). How you own the property should be indicated on your balance sheet as well. Again, we'll dive more into the why when we get to the estate and legal docs section of the playbook.

Perhaps your Real Estate Section of the NWS will look like this:

Real Estate	
71555 Primary - J&D with T.O.D.	$395,000
217 Vacation Home - J&D with T.O.D.	$150,000
555 Rental Home - J&D with T.O.D.	$275,000
615 Office - J&D with T.O.D.	$450,000
Total Real Estate Assets	**$1,270,000**

What about Family Assets?

The Family Assets section of the NWS is a nice catch-all for everything else. Generally though, we tend to think of these assets as personal-use assets that are not expected to increase or even hold their value. Think of these assets as lifestyle assets. They tend to be the toys and creature comforts of our lives.

As a cautionary tale, I've seen more than my share of net worth statements that have very little in short-term assets and equally low on long-term assets while having a lot in the family asset section. See a problem with this? Typically, this person is living for today. While that's not a bad thing, having all your money tied up in depreciating assets like boats, cars, toys and luxury furnishings doesn't exactly create wealth (that's an understatement). In fact, it's a recipe for being broke and potentially having to work your *entire* life.

The family asset section is not where you want much of your wealth. This section typically requires maintenance and usually provides a negative return.

I've seen people cash out retirement accounts so they could continue to make the payment on their brand-new F450 (large truck) that they use for commuting to their office job. That's just a very bad decision and usually not the only one to be made when the all the assets are in the lifestyle section of the Net Worth Statement.

Your Family Assets section of the NWS might look something like this:

Family Assets	
Honda Car - Jack	$11,500
Ford Truck - Diane	$15,500
Household Furnishings	$25,000
Contents of Safe	$11,000
Motorhome	$35,000
Boat	$12,000
Total Family Assets	**$110,000**

Time to Put It All Together

Add all of the totals in the subsections, and you've got a total asset figure. It might look something like this:

Short Term Assets	
PNW C.U. Jack and Diane JTWROS - TOD	$1500.00
The U.S.A. Bank Jack - individually, POD	$1500.00
Cash on hand	$500.00
JPMorgan CD 2% - J&D - JTWROS - TOD	$15,500.00
Total Short Term Assets	**$19,000.00**
Long Term Assets	
ROTH IRA - Jack	$11,500.00
401k - Diane	$150,500.00
Gold Bars	$500.00
Loan to Jack's brother	$15,500.00
Total Long Term Assets	**$178,000.00**
Real Estate	
71555 Primary - J&D with T.O.D.	$395,000
217 Vacation Home - J&D with T.O.D.	$150,000
555 Rental Home - J&D with T.O.D.	$275,000

615 Office - J&D with T.O.D.	<u>$450,000</u>
Total Real Estate Assets	**$1,270,000**
Family Assets	
Honda Car - Jack	$11,500
Ford Truck - Diane	$15,500
Household Furnishings	$25,000
Contents of Safe	$11,000
Motorhome	$35,000
Boat	<u>$12,000</u>
Total Family Assets	$110,000
TOTAL ASSETS	**$1,577,000**

A few comments on the asset side of this hypothetical NWS:

- Given the dollar amount of assets and cash flow needs that go along with maintaining some of those assets like real estate, this couple might have too little in short-term Savings. A general rule of thumb is to have 3–6 months of required spending set aside in short term savings.

- This couple may have too much in real estate relative to the rest of their assets. How about focusing on maxing out the retirement accounts for a few years before adding more real estate? I'd give serious consideration to selling some of the property. Building wealth is about diversification. We often learn that when a concentrated portfolio (could be in Real Estate) suffers due to a poor market condition.

- Lifestyle or family assets are $110,000, almost as much as long-term assets. I'd say we are not dealing with disciplined savers here. It's a balance between fun for today and saving for tomorrow. Right now, fun today seems to be winning.

- On the plus side, it looks like this couple—for the most part—will avoid probate on all the assets. Everything seems to have a TOD or POD, and (we are assuming) the retirement accounts will have beneficiaries listed. We'll revisit this in the estate and legal docs section.

Liabilities and the NWS

"You don't know the power of the dark side."

—Darth Vader

The liability side of the balance sheet IS the dark side. Let's face it—debt is not viewed favorably by most people. Liability is a funny word that has been used creatively to describe people, behaviors, and potential dangers; however, in this book, we'll simply use the word liability to mean a debt (money you owe to someone else). This side of the NWS is the side that you hope to keep to a minimum. After all, we're going to subtract the value of all your debts from your assets to come up with your net worth, so the smaller the number we subtract, the better, right?

While owing someone money does take away from your net worth, it can also add to your net worth in the long run. Let's take a look at how that works.

The first thing we need to discuss is good debt vs. bad debt. I'm going to propose that not all debt is bad. You may already know this. For example, most people carry a mortgage on their home. You can often finance that debt at a fairly low rate. And, for many years, that debt for most people has qualified as a tax deduction on the interest paid. Low interest, tax-deductible interest—good so far. But, how does it add to the net worth? A mortgage, while it is a liability, is paired up with an asset (the home). Owning that home (typically an appreciating asset) has added value to many net worth statements. We won't get into the discussion of whether a home is a good investment or not; you can argue both sides. But I'll stick with it for my example—it's typically a healthy debt to have.

From my perspective, healthy debt means having an interest rate that is lower than *your opportunity cost*. Opportunity cost, a lovely phrase from the world of finance, is simply how much money you could earn by investing in a different 'opportunity.' For example, let's say you have the 'opportunity' to invest in a CD that is paying 7%. OK, that might be your new opportunity cost. If your mortgage is at 4%, you should not pay it off early because you are earning more than the cost of borrowing. Your opportunity cost is higher. That's a healthy debt.

Be careful though, debt is still on the dark side of the NWS. Debt has to be paid, and if you find yourself unable to pay it off—you may lose assets. Don't take on debt you can't pay.

Some other potentially healthy debts might include:

- Student loans at a low rate, lower than your opportunity cost
- Teaser or loss leading loan rates on purchases (0% financing or very low rates)

What about the unhealthy debts? The worst might be <u>credit card or revolving debt</u>. Credit card debt is generally pretty bad stuff. If you don't know this already, <u>please pay off your credit card balances every month. Don't carry a balance.</u> You might argue that a card has a really low rate, and maybe you do the balance transfer game to keep getting low rates. But guess what? You are still are carrying debt to finance your consumer purchases. That means you're living outside of your means, or you were not prepared for an emergency that occurred. Regardless of how you ended up with credit card debt, pay it off and don't get back in it. The credit card companies typically charge really high interest rates, and when you carry a balance, they win. Not you.

Any type of debt that has a high-interest rate is generally bad—even if it's paired up with an asset. A mortgage that might traditionally be thought of as healthy debt, can be unhealthy if it has a high-interest rate. A high-interest debt, to be considered healthy, would require an even higher investment return on the asset that is paired with. A promised high rate of return is going to have a lot of risk and those that chase those high rates of returns by borrowing money usually end off regretting that decision. *High-interest rate debt is bad.*

The HELOC Talk

One type of debt that I actually like as a planning tool and advise people to explore: a home equity line of credit (HELOC). My advice is always to establish the HELOC but don't draw on it. Most recently it seems that many banks and credit unions are wising up to this planning tool and not offering great terms so make sure you do your homework. It's really important to not pay large upfront or back end cost.

Getting a HELOC from your bank or credit union can be 'no to very low' cost. A friend of mine recently paid $139.00 to establish one. The trick is to establish it, but never use it. That way, you have it available to you, but you are not paying any interest because you don't owe anything. *It's just a line of credit available to you.*

Why have it? If you had an absolute emergency, you could draw on it or at least have the option to draw on it. When you have the opportunity to establish a HELOC—you know, when you have good employment income, good credit, good assets, the banks will be happy to lend you money or more accurately, establish that line of credit for you. When you are unemployed, and things just are not going your way, the banks or credit unions really don't want to lend you money or establish you a line of credit. If, however, you had established the line of credit during the good times, it might save you during the bad times.

Establish a HELOC, but don't use it. It's for emergencies when you don't have better options to solve those emergencies.

"Once you start down the high rate path, forever will it dominate your finances."

—*Perhaps Yoda said that?*

It is all about the rate. High = Bad. Low = potentially good, healthy, and happy debt.

Short-Term Liabilities

The short-term liabilities section of the balance sheet is where the unhappy, unhealthy debt usually lives. Let's keep this short in conversation. Don't have debt here. Most people I know have credit cards, the smart people I know have them but don't carry balances. However, if you have credit card debt, you are not alone.

According to creditcards.com author Jeff Herman, the average balance on credit cards is north of $6,000.00. Further, around 40% of the U.S. households have a credit card balance; that's debt they pay high interest on because they don't pay it off each month. Four out of ten people have bad, unhealthy debt. Now that we've identified the problem, let's fix it.

If you are a *'transactor'* or someone who uses the cards but pays them off each month, first of all, congratulations and enjoy the free perks, you don't need to put any balances in the short-term section of the NWS. Just move on!

Auto loans, because they are typically five years or so, can also be put on the short-term section of the NWS. The jury is still out on whether auto loans are healthy or not; it really comes down to the rate. *It's all about the rate!* For example, most of us need cars. But if we have to borrow to get them, hopefully, it's at a good rate.

Lastly, if you owe some money to mom or dad, or siblings or soon to be ex-friends, put it down here as well. While you're listing all your debts, always make notes on the rates. It's all about the rate.

Your short-term section of the NWS might look like this:

Short-Term Liabilities	
Chase Card Jack - 17%	$11,000
BofA Card Diane - 18%	$5000
Honda Loan - 4% J&D	$12,500
Ford Loan - 5% J&D	$5000
Motorhome Loan 9%	$25,000
A loan from Jacks Brother 0%	$5000
Total Short-Term Liabilities	**$63,500**

Long-Term Liabilities

The long-term liabilities section is typically where good debt can live; this is debt that has a life of five years or more. There is no hard and fast rule that says it has to be five years, that's just a number. It could even be a one-year note. If you intended to pay off that one-year note, it would be a short-term debt. But if you were intending on refinancing that note each year for a long-term period, it's long-term.

In this section of the NWS, you would typically have your home loan. As mentioned earlier, your home loan can be considered a healthy debt. **In finance, we use the term 'leverage' to describe the benefit of borrowing at a low cost and investing at a higher return.** Remember to proceed carefully, leverage isn't always good, but you should be aware of the concept.

We might also have student loans in this section; this is a debt that you might consider healthy to have as well. I know many parents who have strived to keep this kind of debt off of their kids' NWS, but I know a lot of successful kids who have some school debt and are working hard because of it!

Your long-term section of the NWS might look like this:

Long-Term Liabilities	
71555 Primary - J&D 4.5%	$225,000
217 Vacation Home - J&D 6.5%	$75,000
555 Rental Home - J&D with 7.5%	$155,000

615 Office – J&D with 7.5%	$150,000
Diane School Loan 4.75%	$52,500
Jack School Loan 2.75%	<u>$75,500</u>
Total Long-Term Debt	**$733,000**

Putting It All Together

<u>Assets minus liabilities equals Net Worth.</u> This is easy stuff but don't brush it off; important stuff!

Most Net Worth Statements are all on one sheet with the assets on one side and the liabilities on the other. Having everything on one sheet is helpful for us to see the big picture at one glance, with a fair amount of detail added. As you picked up on my examples, *I like to add details such as POD and TOD, as well as interest rates either earned or charged on investments and loans.*

The problem with the *'one page'* format is that it's a lot of information to get on one page. You might have to drop some details to get it all on that one page. That's okay—we have a way of dealing with that (we'll cover this later). The benefit of a *'one page'* view is you have the big picture at an easy glance and an easy way to track your progress in managing the business of household finances.

Rather than create a NWS for you with all the details, I'll recap the 'totals' section to give you an idea of how it might look. In your own NWS, you would want as many details listed as you can squeeze into the page. Part of the benefit of a good NWS is a complete list or inventory of what you have. Notice the Assets – Minus Liabilities section in the upper right-hand corner. (That's the number we do all this work for—the Net Worth number).

An abbreviated version of the NWS might look like this:

Net Worth Statement		Net Worth	$780,500
April 1, 2020		(assets - liabilities)	
Short Term Assets	$19,000	Short Term Liabilities	$63,500
Long Term Assets	$178,000	Long Term Liabilities	$733,000
Real Estate	$1,270,000		
Family Assets	$63,500		
Total Assets	**$1,577,000**	**Total Liabilities**	**$796,500**

What Does It All Mean?

<u>First of all, note the date on the upper left. April 1^{st,} 2020.</u> Combine that with the NW figure on the upper right, and you get a meaningful bit of information. The NWS is a snapshot in time. It measures something on a given day, very much like a bathroom scale. As dieters, we'd like our weight to go down over time. And we might track our progress on a graph or spreadsheet or on some app that takes care of it for us—it's the same thing.

A NWS tracks your wealth over time. It tells you how financially healthy you are. The figure of $780,500 is the net worth of the hypothetical example. Getting a starting point of where you are currently and creating a goal to get somewhere else is a very productive approach to building wealth. Add in an action plan on how to get there, and then you really have something!

The Devil Is in the Details

The simple example of the abbreviated NWS omits a lot of detail for the sake of keeping our explanation simple. An actual NWS would carry all of the details previously discuss on it as well or as much as you could get on it. As a result, we end up with a useful tool that tells us a lot more than just our net worth. While the NW figure is like the scale, giving us a snapshot in time of health/wealth, the details in the NWS are like a full-blown blood test giving us much greater detail and insight into not only how our health/wealth is developing, but potentially the direction it is likely to head. Think about the rates being charged on debt vs. the rates being earned on investments—

depending on what is higher, you might be able to forecast a long-term direction for the NWS.

Here are a few examples of how a NWS can help you:

- Identify who owns what asset and who belongs to each liability. This has been very important in the past when it comes to estate planning and is important when there are issues of who controls what in the household financially.

- Identify if your estate is going to be subject to some Estate Taxes.

- Identify who is going to get the assets when you pass away. Remember all the TOD and POD labels.

- Determine if your assets would be subject to PROBATE or not. Often a goal of a household is to avoid probate; having a list of all assets and an indication of registration is the starting point to realizing that goal.

- Illustrate how far you've come year over year or however often you update your NWS (I'm an annual updater, and it's certainly gratifying to see progress over time).

- Understand how leveraged you are. With a few simple calculations, you can see if your debt to asset ratios are acceptable or not.

- Understand how liquid your assets are. If you needed to come up with cash—how fast could you make that happen?

- Recognize if you have too much cash. Is that an issue? If you have a load of cash not earning anything and are well beyond your liquidity needs, then yes.

- Identify how much money you are paying in interest and how much money you are making on yields; this helps in making financial decisions like buying, selling, refinancing, moving, opportunities, etc. etc.

- Examine concentration issues in your wealth. Do you have a large percentage of wealth concentrated in any individual asset (like a building) or asset class (like real estate)? Concentration can create wealth, but there is also a risk that comes with that—See Enron/WorldCom/Lehman (and countless others).

A good NWS can provide some useful insights. It is *not only* the quick bathroom scale measurement of wealth that can help us make effective decisions financially, but it also can tell us a story about what has happened and even help predict what is possibly going to happen. For this reason, I've always called the NWS the cornerstone of good financial planning.

The Cash Flow Statement (or Budget)

The Cash Flow Statement (CFS) might conjure up images of accountants wearing clear green visors and sleeve guards who are madly crunching data for a large corporation. That might sound a little frightening but don't be alarmed. I'll in no way suggest you need to find a green visor. A Cash Flow Statement after all is just a budget. It shows where your money is coming from and where it is going.

Yes, budget—I said it again. (Now you're *really* running for the hills!) When I talk to people about budgets, I get a *glossed-over* look faster than when discussing a prospectus for a bond issue or a proxy vote ballot. Budgeting is not the favorite for many of us.

Budgets don't get a bad rap because nobody understands what it is or how to make one; we just don't want to do it. It's like a mom telling a kid to clean his room—he knows how to do it, but it takes work and he has to confront the messes he's been making. If only that kid understood that once he cleaned his room, keeping it clean is just a matter of simple maintenance and good habits like putting his clothes in the hamper rather than the floor! A budget is similar, once we have one it's easy to maintain and we can keep it intact by creating good habits.

The Scale vs. the Food Log

One way to view a budget is to think of a it similar to a nutrition plan. Income is like nutrition for the body and bills are like burning that energy. It's a matter of looking at how you are getting income/energy by looking at your revenue/food-intake. Then, it looks at your expenses/energy use by looking at your bills/exercise activity.

If the Net Worth Statement is the bathroom scale, then the Cash Flow Statement is the diet and exercise log. The NWS shows us where we are at the moment. It's like our weight. Granted, we can see more detail by looking closer as modern scales can show us more details than just the weight, like body fat, water weight, etc. The Cashflow statement tells us *what we are doing to impact the NWS*, just like the diet and exercise log tells us what we are doing to impact the scale.

> The Cash Flow Statement shows us what changes will happen on our Net Worth Statement just like a diet and exercise log shows us what changes are going to happen on the scale. If you want to move your Net Worth Number, start with the Cash Flow Statement.

If I spent my days spending more money than I was making, for example, what how would that look on my CFS and NWS? Well, my CFS would show that I'm at a deficit each month. In other words, I am living outside my means, at least temporarily. How does that impact my NWS? At least temporarily, my net worth figure will likely head south. Everything else being equal, if we spend more than we make, we are going to be diminishing our assets and or taking on debt. The impact, as we know, is a weaker NWS. Follow this path, and you could eventually be broke. Or, worse yet always be broke!

There might be exceptions to the idea laid out above. We could have unrealized real estate gains, a stock portfolio that is appreciating, an inheritance that has or is coming, or any sudden windfall. All of these things could keep the NWS moving in the correct direction. And, running a deficit (spending more than you are making) on the CFS isn't necessarily a bad thing for everyone. Some people have a very well-articulated goal for doing so— "let the last check to the undertaker bounce!" Or, "I'd see the money be spent or put to work before my passing." So, it's OK to run a deficit yes, but if your goal is to build wealth on the NWS, you need to be aware of how the CFS affects your net worth *and* that running a deficit is generally going to have a negative impact.

I had a personal trainer once tell me, "Ben, it's diet and exercise that gets you in shape. If you want to lose weight, you have to eat right and burn calories." Mick was right, and I moved the scale in the right direction by focusing on the diet and exercise log. The same advice is true for the NWS. In general, if you want to move the net worth figure up, you need to be taking in more than you are letting out. The NWS *is* the scale, and the CFS is the diet and exercise log!

Details or Big Picture?

As you prepare your own CFS, you can gravitate to one end of the spectrum where you are extremely detailed and adding every single bill down to the penny. Imagine the accuracy of reporting and the truths that you will learn by really taking a hard look at your income and expenses. How very exciting that is for some people!

The downside to such a dive into details method is probably that if you spend a day every month getting into finite details of how much you spend via on-demand movies in the documentary category or amazon purchases exclusively for the garage; you might find the CFS takes a lot of your time. The more accurate you want the CFS, the more time it is going to take you.

On the other end of the spectrum, you might have bigger picture preference and want a rough idea of whether or not you are living within your means (although your NWS might tell you that) and an approximate of where you are spending your money. You might lean towards lumping all credit card expenses together and lumping all utilities together. This approach is quick and easy. When it's needed, the Cash Flow Statement can be recreated relatively easily with little effort. After all, it's more of an approximation.

While the bigger picture preference method is fast, requires little updating, it doesn't have the finer details that might lend to better decisions. Having all of your utilities lumped together might not let you know that you are spending three times as much on cable as your Netflix, Hulu, and Prime combined. That knowledge might give you the insight to cut the cord because when you think about it, you hardly ever watch cable. Having credit card expenses lumped together might not illustrate that you spend ten times the amount of money eating out than at the grocery store. As that becomes obvious, you might decide to explore some cooking classes to cut back on expenses.

If you are living within your means and are comfortable with where you are—you might not need the details. It's probably why those fast-metabolic types might not count calories or log exercise. It might just come naturally to them. And, for the financially fit, sometimes spending hours looking at the details might be a bad use of time. But, like fine-tuned athletes we recognize that there is always room for improvement, and we do gain an edge by looking at the details or hiring consultants to do it for us.

Regardless of where you land on the continuum from details to big picture, do what works best for you when it comes to creating your Cash Flow Statement. The fact that you have one will put you one step ahead of most people.

Tips and Tricks to Maximize the Benefits of the CFS

I do not doubt that taking a hard look at your CFS can enlighten anyone, but the question of how much time to put into it depends on your time available and your goals. But, for anyone undertaking the project, here are some tips and tricks to add more useful information to even the most detailed of Cash Flow Statements.

1. **Use percentages for each line item.** It's easy to do and knowing how much of your income as a percentage goes to debt service, for example, can be very useful. You might know before a lender if you are going to get a loan.

2. **Clearly label your information.** If it's Jack's income stream, name it. If Jack were pass away, Diane might want to assess what will continue after he is gone.

3. **Note Income that will come in the future.** For example, in the labeling area, I might say Social Security benefit payments at age 65 or 62 are $xxxx.xx. Or pension at age 65 is $xxxx.xx. It's another great spot to track those figures. As my Cash Flow Statement transitions over to the work optional lifestyle, I can see how well my expenses are going to be covered.

4. **If you have a loan or source of income that ends at a certain date, make a note.** That really expensive car loan you took out that is ending in six months is going to have a huge impact on your CFS. Your CFS should be telling you that story.

Benefits of the Cash Flow Statement for Those Who Take over

Your Cash Flow Statement is the diet and exercise log of financial health. So how does that help those who take over for us when we need them? I have seen some benefits to adding details for those that are picking up the pieces. Call it a post-mortem autopsy for the finances. Having a good look at the comings and goings of income and expenses can be very helpful.

The Cash Flow Statement as well as the Net Worth Statement, can be of help if you're taking over your parents' finances because they are no longer capable of handling these responsibilities, or they have passed on. Or you want to make sure that your kids are not stuck scrambling for answers when and if something were to happen to you.

The Cash Flow Statement can give those who are now in charge, a list of all your bills. That's a great starting point for figuring out how to manage those relationships going forward or how to quickly end them if needed. No sense in continuing to pay for the premium cable package when you are not going to use it, but you certainly might want to make sure the electric bill is being paid. Credit Card payments (whether full payments or partial) that show up on the

Cash Flow Statement are a great hint that we need to contact these companies and either change authorizations or end the credit.

On the income side of the Cash Flow Statement, many listed items like pensions and Social Security retirement benefits will stop automatically when a death certificate is filed. Large insurance companies, pensions, and of course branches of the government monitor those things pretty carefully—much like we should monitor the expense side to ensure we don't continue to pay for things after we shouldn't. They view the payments being sent to us as an expense and they do a great job making sure that they don't send them any longer than they need to. We should do the same.

In the event of death, some things on the income side might need our immediate attention. For example, distributions from IRAs or investment accounts might need our involvement to stop them from getting sent out. Sometimes getting IRA distributions after death might negatively impact the tax implications of the deceased estate. Sometimes, automatic investment withdrawals that continue after someone is deceased can cause tax problems. Sometimes, those distributions would have been better left reinvested for the benefit of the heirs. If the distributions from a highly appreciated piece of property were being sent out, we might want to stop the sale of those assets and elect to get a step up in basis instead. That creates tax efficiency. The point is this, simply knowing who to contact and how to start a conversation can move the resources in the right direction.

What the CFS Looks Like and How to Create One

A CFS is something that is certainly not a mystery to Google. Do a quick search, and you will find what seems to be an endless amount of variations already created. Do you own a PC with MS office? If so, templates in Excel exist. Do you own a Mac with Numbers? If so, templates exist! And then, of course, there are several web-hosted online applications, various apps available, and then there is the old fashion handwritten and hand calculated version. Regardless of what you use, it's going to get the job done, and since there are so many variations, it's a matter of preference.

A few ideas I like in a CFS are as follows:

- Keep it simple enough to easily update (the more of a chore it is to update, the less likely it will get done).

- On the left side of the page show all income and on the right side show expenses (this separates the two more clearly).

- Break income and expenses into fixed and variable (this lets you know what you can count on and what might fluctuate).

- Don't forget to note Social Security benefit payments for future consideration as well as pensions and other streams of income. (you could do the same with expected payments that might be made in the future).

- Add notes—it will add color! (example, when a loan ends).

A cash flow statement might look like this:

Cash Flow Statement	Jack and Diane	April 20, 2020	
Monthly Amounts	**Deficit or Surplus**	= income - expenses	**$1000.00**
Fixed Income		Fixed Expenses	
Salary Jack	5000.00	Mortgage	2000.00
Salary Diane	5000.00	Vacation Mortgage	1500.00
SS at 65 Jack 2500		Office Mortgage	2500.00
SS at 65 Diane 2500		Student Loans	200.00
Pension D at 65 2500		Car Loan (ends 2025)	225.00
Rental Income	1500.00	Total Fixed	6425.00
Annuity Payments	1000.00		
Total Fixed	**12,500.00**	Variable Expenses	
		Credit Card Pymts	
Variable Income		Entertainment	750.00

Stock Dividends	350.00	Taxes	3150.00
Gifts From Aunty	1000.00	College Savings	300.00
Side Biz Income	500.00	Retirement Savings	500.00
Total Variable	**1850.00**	Household Shopping	1500.00
		Gas	250.00
Total Income	**14,350.00**	Utilities	300.00
		Insurance	175.00
		Total Variable	**3925.00**
		Total Expenses	**13,350.00**

Add all the expenses up and subtract them from the income. The example above shows a surplus of $1000.00 per month. A good cash flow statement would show a surplus each month. A surplus can go to short term savings, short term savings can go to long term savings or pay off debt. Either one is good for the Net Worth Statement and a great way to create wealth.

Company Generated Financial Statements

I'm going to propose that you *only* save a single recent copy for each of the companies with which you do business. File them in the financial section of your playbook and replace them every year or each time you have a significant change. The rest, I'd like you to shred! Read on.

Most people might consider the statements they get in the mail (assuming they haven't switched them over to email) from the bank, investment company, 401k, and other companies similar to actual financial statements like a net worth statement or cash flow Statement. And, in a sense, they are correct. They deal with finances, and they are statements. However, they are typically just statements for one financial relationship exclusively. Our NWS and CFS give us glimpse of everything at once while company generated statements only deal with one company. Think of company generated statements as supporting details to the much more important NWS and CFS. So, what do we do with those supporting details?

Common Ways to Deal with Company Generated Statements

When most people get company generated statements, they tend to either shred them right away, open them and file them away, or leave them unopened and bring them to the tax or financial guy they know. All three methods have some pitfalls that I think we can address.

The problem with the first method (just shreds them right away) is that you might be missing something important like a big account value change that could concern you. You might also be destroying a copy of something that you might need to prove you have, or you might need the account information to call a representative or have the account number available. This method is quick, but it's somewhat negligent.

The second method (open them and file them away) is one where you might be looking for changes in the statements and then storing them because they have information you might need. But how often do you purge the filing cabinet? If you are like most people, I know you end up with years and years and boxes upon boxes of statements that you eventually either pass onto your kids or you give up and take to a shredding company. This method, while attempting to be responsible with statements by saving them, is only creating a problem for down the road.

The third method (bring them to your trusted advisor) might lead to a great review of the statements and a quick, experienced set of eyes to relieve you of the responsibility of understanding the statement. But it might not be the best use of time for either party. Plus, you have to usually pack up and schlep the stuff into someone's office. Let's talk about how to take ownership of these statements. But first let's discuss why to keep them.

Why Keep Financial Statements at All?

You want at least one copy of every statement you get from an investment company, but why? First, you might have to prove that you actually have the asset (or liability). I hope you never have to prove to a financial institution you are dealing with that you have business with them. That probably won't happen, but you might have to prove to one financial institution that you have assets at another financial institution. Remember, because of privacy laws, companies can't call and ask each other questions about you. You have to provide them with proof. Think about a refinance or applying for a loan, typically, you have to provide copies of statements, and typically they want recent statements.

Second, it's nice to have a copy of these company generated financial statements in case you have to call the company. You can usually find the address, phone number, account number, and other vital information on page one.

But, do you need to keep *all* the statements that come in the mail? No Way. I'm telling you that is pure craziness! Just keep a recent copy of each of the statements for the companies that you have a relationship with and get rid of all the rest. You will have the latest information you need, and you will rid yourself of the hoarding habit of saving everything that comes in the mail because you don't know how to deal with it. Imagine having all that filing cabinet space freed up for meaningful things like family photos and dream files!

So, when a statement comes in the mail, what do you do? Do you put it in the book every time and replace the old one? About once a year or anytime there are significant changes replace the old statement with a new one. In the meantime, open the statements, review them for anything out of the ordinary, and then... right to the shredder! Clean, easy and touched only once.

But It Can't Be That Easy Because…

Wait, you might say, "I like to go back in time and see what happens from period to period."

Well time traveler, that's why we update the NWS once a year or as often as you have the energy. And if you need to see what happens from month to month fine. It's just a lot of work. I'll tell you though, seeing what happens from year to year or decade to decade is much more gratifying than every month. Review statements every month fine, but think a little longer term for the 'are we making progress' question.

You might say, "What if I want to review the finite details of what happened in my account two winters ago, and I've shredded the statements already?"

Great question, as this will occasionally come up. The good news is that you are going to be hard-pressed to find a company that cannot generate statements for you for the past few decades. You might have to pay for it, but it will be cheaper in the long run than creating a hoarding habit!

"What about 'basis' – my tax professional said it's important, didn't she?" (Basis is what is referred to as your taxable investment in an Asset—what you paid for it. Ultimately it determines how much gain or loss you might have when selling the asset and that translates into how much taxes you may have to pay).

If you still get a statement from a company and you are worried about if they are keeping track of basis, stop what you are doing right now and head to the phone—this an easy one to figure out. Basis (again, this is fancy accountant talk for what you paid for something) is now required to be tracked for you. If you they don't have it because you perhaps transferred the asset to them and the basis wasn't reported from the transferring firm, call them up and figure it out. If that's what you are saving statements for, you no longer have to.

Once a company starts to track basis for you, the idea hanging onto that original confirmation of purchase just seems silly, doesn't it? The additional benefit is that when you dispose of the asset the company who has the basis will include it right on the 1099 for the tax professionals.

How the Financial Statement Section of the Playbook Ties into the Rest of the Book

- **The Goal Objectives and Projections Section** of the Playbook has a lot to do with the Net Worth Statement. Most people have financial goals. The Cash Flow Statement often indicates where your money is going. From that snapshot, we can see how it is reflected in your Wealth Purpose Statement.

- **The Estate Planning Section** ties directly into the Net Worth Statement. When your administrator is handling your estate, they will certainly be happy to see that you've organized all of your statements in one spot. And, as you plan for the distribution of your assets during your life, your advisors will be benefited from having quick access to your financial information all in one spot!

- **The Insurance section of your Playbook** is all about making sure your assets are protected, whether that's your home, car, properties (all on your Net Worth Statement), or your Human capital (all on your Cash Flow Statement).

- **The Tax section of your Playbook** is going to tie into the tax efficiency of your assets and liability on your Net Worth Statement as well as your income and potential tax deductions on your Cash Flow Statement. Think of the Tax section as some detailed analysis of how efficient your NWS and CFS are operating from the tax perspective.

- **The Performance section** is all about measuring how your Net Worth Statement and Cash Flow Statement are working. These two documents are the building blocks of financial management.

- Finally, **the Social Security and Pension section** is going to impact not only what the Cash Flow Statement is going to look like (your payments clearly will show up here), but depending on what your goals/objectives are and the health of your Net Worth Statement, they may create an asset on the Net Worth Statement itself (see lump sum distribution options).

From the Playbook Players

The Hoarder of Statements

Can you imagine saving nearly everything that came in the mail? No, of course not. But what about everything that seems to be important or financially relevant? Maybe. We've run into several clients who have adopted this strategy before meeting us and then changing to the Playbook strategy. The justification is something like "I'm not sure what it is, I just got it in the mail so better to be safe than sorry. I'll just store it."

We recently met the niece of a deceased man who had, because he didn't know if it was worth saving or not, saved most financial mailings in the last several decades. The niece brought in box after box of old statements, pension benefit award letters, old insurance policies, and countless other items deemed to be worthy of the collection. We were floored! We couldn't possibly go through every statement she had.

We had to create a system for her to implement. It amounted to sorting various statements in piles by company or account number. Then we assisted with tracking down each of the companies to find out if an account existed or if a policy was still valid or if an old stock certificate was worth anything. It took weeks, and it amounted to very little. There was no hidden gem.

Could you imagine how much easier her life would have been if she was given a nice Net Worth Statement so she could tell right away what her deceased uncle's estate was all about? Or if she didn't have to deal with the over-whelming statement issue in the first place because he only saved what was most meaningful and most recent!

Registration Mess

Sometimes people go to great lengths and expense to get their estate planning taken care of at one point in time, only to find it isn't effective in the long run. We often see new clients who may have a family trust set up, but all the new accounts they've opened in the last few years are individually owned. For most people that defeats the purpose of the trust. The Net Worth Statement is a chance to review all the registrations to make sure they are up to date.

One particular new client we visited with had relationships with five different banks and each one of them had a substantial amount of assets. Further, each of the registrations at the bank were individually owned, not in the trust that turned out to have been set up. After interviewing the new client, it turned out the trust was set up to reduce potential estate tax and to avoid probate. Fortunately, we were able to get the registrations corrected on all of the accounts. Had we not, this client's beneficiaries would have surely faced a great deal more in estate taxes as well as probate cost, time and frustration.

CHAPTER THREE

Estate Planning and Legal Documents

Welcome to the estate planning and legal documents section of your Playbook. For many, this is one of the most neglected areas of your adult life. If you haven't addressed this area of your financial planning, don't feel too bad. Surprisingly few people take the time to do proper estate planning.

I've heard that most people don't want to face their own mortality and so when the topic of estate planning comes up, they bury the idea. Each time the topic is resurrected, they are quick to bury it again. I think I can agree with that statement, but I also tend to think that people have a preconceived notion that estate planning is much harder than it really is. For most people, it's going to be surprisingly easy.

In this section I'll write about what goes into the Estate Planning and Legal Documents section of the Playbook and we'll discuss the meaning and purpose of various legal articles. By the end of this chapter, you should feel a whole lot better about this area of your life.

Before proceeding any further, though, I'm not an attorney, and I'm not giving you legal advice. However, I'm going to tell you what I've seen work and not work with my clients over the last two plus decades. If you have any doubts or confusion by the end of this section, please consult an attorney.

The Contents

The following items would be appropriate for inclusion in this section of your Playbook:

- Estate planning documents like a will or a trust
- Powers of Attorney (POAs)
- Health Care POAs or Advance Directives
- Burial arrangements and last wishes
- Legal contracts you hold with another party like employment contracts
- Property registration records, like Transfer on Death registration
- The Schedule A – personal property disposition list
- Beneficiary Review Form
- Love letters to the family or Legacy Letters
- A list of not so obvious people places and things

As with any section in your Playbook, you can add items that you think make sense. The framework of the Playbook is to provide options on how you deal with your issues. This book, about the Playbook, is to remind you that those issues exist and to make sure that you address them.

Estate Planning Documents Like a Will or Trust

Let's tackle the big one right away. The Will, or in the event you've got a need for it, the Trust. Having these documents stored in your playbook is a must. When you are working with your advisors, you will want them to be familiar with your estate plan. Since these two documents will control most of your estate, you will want to be able to furnish them with a copy. In the event you run into your early demise or a joint demise, having these documents available in your Playbook will greatly assist those left behind in sorting out your affairs. Even if you have another estate planning folder, please remember that the Playbook is all-encompassing and meant to be the resource for all of your financial affairs. You should not omit these documents from your Playbook.

Original Documents or Copies?

I once heard an attorney claim that you could draft a will on the back of a napkin, and a copy of that napkin could satisfy some courts under the right circumstances. In my practice as an advisor, setting up numerous Trust accounts for clients has never required me to present an original Trust document. A copy gets the job done for trust accounts to get set up and often it's just a certification of trust, a one or two page document that has some details needed for the account, that is required.

Don't get rid of the original though. Some courts would prefer the original and they are probably less contestable than a copy. But to the question of do you keep it in the Playbook? I'd suggest not. I'd suggest you keep the original documents stored somewhere like in a safe or safe deposit box. You only need to have working copies of the documents in your Playbook, not the originals.

With your originals neatly tucked away in a safe, or a similar secure location, make a note on the copies indicating where the originals are located. Don't make the process of settling your estate a mystery for those doing it. Give them a clue.

Also, give yourself a clue as well by taking the time to write a one-page summary outlining the important stipulations of each lengthy document you add to your Playbook. For example, for the will, you might make a note of:

1. Who is in charge of your affairs? (and in what order do the executors follow?)

2. Who gets what's leftover? (the beneficiaries)

3. What special provisions, if any, does the document have? (like the kids only get money if they attend college or after 30 years of age)

We do this so that the long-winded legalese that it takes to draft such documents doesn't have to be reviewed by you each time you want to refresh your memory. The one page note is only for you and potentially for your executor but won't have any impact on the document itself. For that reason, if our attorneys don't draft the one pager for us, we can feel free to draft one without any worry about altering the outcome of our careful estate planning.

A Quick Review of the Difference between a Will and a Trust

The Will is a document that assists with the probate process. This document is a way for you to communicate your wishes to the probate court. Many people don't want probate because they have either dealt with it or heard stories about the process being expensive and time-consuming. Again, a Will assists with the probate process. If you are planning on a Will being used, you are planning on probate.

I've heard so many people over the years talk about the Will they got set up so their kids wouldn't have to deal with probate. Because there seems to be such a misunderstanding about the document, I cannot help but mention it here several times. In my family estate plan, I don't want a Will if I want to avoid probate.

A Will guides the probate process, and if I have a Will and think it will be used, I'm assuming things *will* be probated.

A pour-over will, however, is something that is a part of my estate plan. It acts as a safety net and hopefully won't be used. But, if by some chance I miss something that would otherwise avoid probate through proper title and registration, it would tell the courts what I'd like to have happen to the asset. It usually points back to the trust work that was set up.

What Is a Trust?

The Trust is a probate bypassing solution amongst other things. Now is another good time to state, I'm not a lawyer. The depth of legal planning that can exist in complicated estate work is not for the faint of heart. That is truly better off left to the professional, and I'll do just that. Estate planning and a deep dive into the tools used are outside the scope of this book. However, for the sake of your Playbook, I'll briefly explain a few benefits of various kinds of trust documents.

First, a trust allows assets to pass outside of probate. It does this by titling or registering things in the name of the trust. So, instead of belonging to John and Jane Doe, the asset now belongs to The John and Jane Doe Family Trust. Then, the trust has directions to leave the assets to designated beneficiaries after John and Jane have passed. It is just a simple set of instructions that allows a predetermined beneficiary to exist, so no probate is needed.

Second, a Trust can divide up an otherwise larger estate into two separate estates. Why in the world would you have wanted to do this? Besides the fact that many assets coming together often involves a second, third, or more marriages, a couple may want to create separate estates to minimize or entirely avoid estate taxes. I'll leave the finer points for others to tackle, but for now, know that if you have an estate tax problem, you are probably going to get an A/B trust. Often referred to morbidly as A – above ground and B – below ground.

Third, to some degree, you get to control assets from the grave or when you are not capable of making decisions. The trust can outline what needs to happen with the assets you place in that trust and the distribution of those assets. Often, a benefactor, the person creating and funding the trust, might want to put assets in a trust that place restrictions on the beneficiary getting access to those funds. Think of an adult with a special needs child that should have the assets carefully distributed on their behalf and for their benefit. Or consider the parents who have that wild and crazy kid waiting to inherit a big chunk of change. Those parents may choose to make sure that their son or daughter graduates from a four year university before receiving an inheritance.

A Trust is a perfectly legal, appropriate, and very thoughtful tool. There are so many types of Trusts you can set up, and they can do such wonderful things for you. Every diligent planner would have a trust if it weren't for the cost of creating one. The cost is much more than the ink and paper. While we'd like to think the online resources that exist might be a good solution for our problems, the truth of the matter is that the world of estate planning and trust planning is evolving and much deeper and complex than many people give it credit for. For that reason, we hire attorneys to do the work for us. And, that's where the real cost comes in. Well earned but potentially expensive.

Trust Alternatives

Another option to the Trust for avoiding probate that is potentially less expensive is to simply add beneficiaries on all of your assets ahead of time, thus avoiding probate. This strategy is often referred to as the Poor Man's Trust but we'll call it the Prudent Person's Trust. This strategy doesn't cost much other than time, and for many people, it is a great strategy. The issue is that it requires some diligence to make sure that you have dotted the I's and crossed the T's. Tie this in with the Net Worth Statement and Beneficiary Review Form to document and doublecheck the process, and you might have an estate that bypasses probate because everything already has instructions on it to pass to certain people or entities. Let's take a closer look.

How Does the Prudent Person Trust Work?

The Will assists the probate court by telling the court who you want the assets to go to, and the Trust moves the assets into a new registration with designated beneficiaries, or heirs already listed, the Prudent Person Trust concept just cuts out the trust but adds beneficiaries to the assets as they are currently registered. Let me give you an example:

Let's say Pat Jones owns a bank account at XYZ Bank with a balance of $5000. When Pat dies (sorry, Pat), the bank account would not be accessible by anyone without a court order the bank isn't going to take the liability of giving it to the wrong person. If they give it to the wrong person, they might be sued and have to pay the $5000.00 to the right person. Even if you knew the bank manager and he knew who your beneficiaries *should be* it's not that easy. Banking institutions have very strict policies about distributing funds and for very good reasons. The bank can't presume to know what you want to happen to your assets when you die, so probate must be involved.

If you don't have a will, then the court uses its own predefined process called intestate. Each state has its own set of criteria. The intestate process tries to do a fair job of distributing that $5000.00 as they think you might have wanted. Generally, they are going to look for a spouse, then kids, then close relatives.

Intestate isn't a bad thing; it is just a process in place for the intention of doing the right thing. Most people would be fine with intestate because they generally want the same thing that the intestate process would give them. However, each state is potentially different, and why leave it up to chance? Further, intestate is going to take time, and you are ultimately leaving it in the hands of someone else. Things could get fouled up, and you don't have much customization of how things will work out. So, many people create a will.

If you have a Will, that's great; that document will assist with the probate process. If your Will says, "Give it all to my kid Bill," then that is what's going to happen. Sounds great, but you paid to draft a Will likely, and now your estate is going to be tied up for probably six months while the court asks if any creditors think some of that $5000.00 belongs to them. Further, your heirs might be paying a lot more than the $5000.00 to hire an attorney to file the correct paperwork. Or, skip the attorney and learn the paperwork process yourself by spending potentially several frustrating weeks or more trying to understand what is needed. It's not fun. If you don't have gray hair already, you'll get it from the probate process—especially if you are attempting it yourself. If you find yourself in that position and you can afford it, and hopefully it's for more than $5000.00, you should hire an attorney.

Now, let's say you have a bank account, but the ownership is by the Trust you set up. Pat Jones Trust Account owns the bank account at XYZ Bank with a balance of $5000. When Pat dies, the Trust still exists.

If you happen to have someone else as the current trustee or person in charge of the Trust, nothing really changes at all. If you are like most people and just set up this Trust to distribute the assets at your death, then it is going to work like this. The person named to manage the affairs of the Trust, the successor trustee named in the trust documents, is going to go to the bank and provide them with a copy of your death certificate and then the bank is going to follow the directions provided by the Trust documents and ultimately the instructions of the successor trustee. The Trust instructions probably said something like, "Give the asset to Bill when I die." And that's exactly what the bank will do. No court is needed, no court order is required, no probate, no delay, and most likely no cost at all. The reason that Trust worked so well is that there was no liability on the part of the bank.

The bank only needs to follow the instructions given by the Trust and Trustee. The bank most likely can't be sued if it is following instructions already predetermined by the Trust and created when the person who set up the Trust (grantor) was alive and signed over the assets to the Trust. There is simply no liability, and the bank has a clear set of instructions on what to do. Easy!

Now, Let's See How This Account Works with the Prudent Person Trust Concept

We are going to use something called Payable on Death (P.O.D.) in the following example: Pat Jones owns an account at XYZ Bank with P.O.D. instructions to Bill Jones. Under this registration type, when Pat passes, Bill will go to the bank with a copy of the death certificate, and the bank will 'pay' the $5000.00 to Bill. Done. No court, no probate, no court order, no cost, no waiting. It's all easy as pie.

Just like the Trust example above, under this scenario, the bank has instructions on file that Pat created when Pat was alive. The bank has no liability or risk of getting it to the wrong person because Pat told them exactly what the plan was ahead of time. The Bank has to follow the instructions you have already set up or they would have liability.

Imagine having a set of instructions on file with all of your accounts and assets. Imagine that these instructions told the bank or title companies who to give the assets to in the event you die. If you can do this, you can avoid probate on all your assets, and you don't have to create a trust. Just provide instructions ahead of time for all of your assets. That is the Prudent Person Trust.

Registration Types Reviewed

We covered registration types in the Financial Statements section pretty extensively, but let's look at some more. Here's a list of common registration types that specifically avoid probate and how to use them.

- **Payable On Death (P.O.D.):** Add this to a bank account or any 'cash money-market account' typically offered by a bank or credit union. (You often have to ask for this yourself.)

Depending on where you bank, the bank employee, although well-intentioned, might not have the insight to suggest you think about what happens when you die.

- **Transfer On Death (T.O.D.):** Add this to assets other than bank accounts that can be transferred to someone at death. The difference here is that P.O.D. pays out on death. In other words, the account will be closed, and the cash will be handed over. With a T.O.D., the asset still exists, but it has a new owner (e.g., a piece of real estate like a house, a stock, or gold mining rights). This method allows the beneficiary to have the decision to keep the asset or liquidate it if the opportunity exists to do so.

- **Joint Tenants With Rights Of Survivorship (J.T.W.R.O.S.):** This registration type allows for more than one person to own an asset at the same time, but when one of the parties passes away the ownership transfers to the remaining parties. So, you could own a bank account, or a piece of real estate, together and have probate avoidance set up if one of the parties dies. You can use this with multiple people. For example, John, Jane, Jack, and Jill could all own an account together and be four equal owners. If John dies, then Jane, Jack, and Jill now become the three equal owners.

Accounts That Should Naturally Avoid Probate

Some types of assets, like life insurance, retirement accounts, and annuities, are set up from the start to avoid probate. But hold the horses a sec, these accounts only avoid probate because they have beneficiary designations built into the application process. So, when you sign up for the annuity, life insurance, or retirement account, the people processing the work require you to designate who it goes to if you pass away. Is it a law that these accounts bypass probate? Heck no! They are often subject to probate. But wait, you say, you just suggested they would naturally avoid probate? What gives?

While these types of accounts are set up to include beneficiaries and avoid probate, the companies that set up these accounts do not maintain beneficiary designations for you. In other words, they don't update the beneficiaries on your behalf. They can't. So, if your beneficiaries are no longer alive when you pass away, the asset may go to probate. Wow, that's a bummer. You've got an asset that is supposed to bypass probate, but because the beneficiary listed on file no longer exists, what choice does the company that has the assets have? They have no choice but to only act on a court order at this point. They can't presume to know what you would have wanted instead of the original beneficiary.

Even if an account is meant to avoid probate by design, it won't, given the right, or rather very wrong circumstances. So, for that reason, we'll discuss this later in this section, having a Beneficiary Review Form is a great way to manage and track beneficiary designations on your assets to make sure you have the I's dotted.

Common Questions and Answers

Why tackle estate planning at all—doesn't it just sort itself out?

Estate planning is typically for the benefit of those we leave behind, the beneficiaries. When we lose a loved one, it can be overwhelming, and the added stress and pressure to wrap up an estate can be very challenging. When families are wrapping up an estate, this is often the time when I see siblings stop talking to each other. Dealing with a messy estate compounds all the emotions and stresses of losing a loved one. Most people don't want their loved ones to struggle with the process, and we try to do everything we can in advance to ease things for those taking over. That is a big part of estate planning.

What about just adding the kids to the account as owners?

I hate this idea. You, for one thing, are gifting your kids' half of whatever you put in this account. Let's say for example you sell your house for $500k and deposit that $500k into your checking jointly held with your kid. Technically, you just gifted your kid $250k. Why does this matter? You are only allowed to gift a small amount each year without filing a gift tax return. In addition to the filing requirement, anything beyond that small amount may reduce your ability to ultimately avoid estate taxes. So, not only do you have to file another return, the gift tax return, but in addition you've just offset your unified credit amount by the gift. That sounds a little complex but what it amounts to is your estate will now have an increased likelihood of being subject to estate tax when it is settled. That translates into less money for the heirs and more money for the IRS.

Second, if your kid gets in a car wreck or any other sort of havoc and finds himself in a lawsuit, that $500k that you just deposited and is half his, now is subject to the lawsuit. Your kid could cost you $250k of your assets because he got sued, and you made him a joint owner on your checking account. Despite this risk, I see people add kids to accounts all the time to avoid probate. The better solution, make them a signer if you want them to be able to pay bills, and a P.O.D. (Payable on Death) beneficiary if you want to avoid probate, but NOT an owner.

I don't have to worry about beneficiary reviews because my Will takes care of all that, right?

I hear this question all the time. However, the way your Will is going to deal with this is by having the assets probated. Further, if your beneficiary designation has your ex-spouse on an account, but your Will says to leave everything to your children, what do you think is going to happen to the asset? It's going to go to your ex-spouse, end of the story. There might be some legal juggling that occurs, but the company holding the asset is going to turn it over to the ex-spouse. Those are the instructions they have on file. Regardless of what your will says. Remember, they have to follow the set of instructions they have on file.

Do you want to avoid Probate?

For most of you, yes. Now, some attorneys and smart minds will point out that the probate process not only relieves companies of the liability of giving assets to the wrong people, but it also protects your assets from claims of creditors after the probate process. So, once the six months or so has expired, and the probate process is over, potential creditors have a harder time placing claim on the assets. Publicly announcing the probate of an estate is supposed to give creditors a chance to go before the courts and claim their share. We see these announcements in the paper. Once that chance is over, creditors don't have as much of an argument to claim assets.

Power of Attorney (P.O.A.)

A P.O.A. gives another party the right to make decisions on your behalf. Having a P.O.A. is often much more beneficial to a family than having a Will because it deals with the event of when we are unable to manage our affairs while we are alive. If we are laid up in the hospital in a coma, who is going to manage our assets? If we die, our assets go to the beneficiaries, but not until we die. The P.O.A. deals with transferring the ability to make decisions to someone else while we are still alive. But, because we don't want to make this decision lightly, it's often a great idea to consult with a competent legal mind that can help you navigate the pros and cons of such a decision. See an attorney.

A Durable Power of Attorney is one that is established and is effective from inception until it's revoked. It could be useful for making various types of decisions and those often cover a lot of ground. Often the scope of decisions that can be made by the designated P.O.A. is included in the document. This type of P.O.A. can grant power immediately and for a broad scope. As a result, you have to be very careful with this one.

A Springing Power of Attorney is one that comes into effect once a certain thing occurs, usually a health related issue. This type of P.O.A. often requires one or more doctors to get involved and verify the health-related issue has occurred. From our practice, this type of P.O.A. can be frustratingly slow to implement.

Having a copy of your P.O.A. in your Playbook makes it accessible to those that need to get a copy of it. Most companies do not require an original copy. In fact, I'm not sure I know of any that do. Often, a P.O.A. will not have an expiration date, but the person granted the power might have to certify themselves that the form is still valid. We just had this happen recently when a P.O.A. was more than five years old. The counterparty wanted verification by having the person who was granted the power to sign a notarized affidavit indicating the power was still good. Imagine—the person granting the power didn't have to confirm permission, but rather the person receiving the power had that authority. That struck us as an odd policy.

Health Care POA's and Advance Directives

A Health Care P.O.A. names a person to make decisions for you regarding your health care. Similar to a P.O.A. but specific for health. Usually, this happens when you can no longer make these decisions for yourself. Imagine being sick to the point where you couldn't make decisions. One suggestion coming from a Playbook Pioneer was to have the designated person keep a copy of the Power in their glovebox. In the event they were rushing to the hospital to advise over your health, they'd have the appropriate paperwork at their fingertips.

An Advanced Directive, often called a living will, is a set of instructions that communicates to your healthcare providers what your wishes are. Rather than naming a person, this form names what actions you would like to have taken place. For example, DNR or organ donation wishes.

Burial Arrangements and Last Wishes

Many people take the time to prearrange the handling of their bodies when they pass. Often, this is a prepaid arrangement for burial, plots, or other services to be rendered. Where else would you keep records of this type of transaction other than your Playbook?! Not only do you have a specific place where you've stored proof, but your beneficiaries, who will likely be handling these arrangements on your behalf, have a logical place to find a record of your efforts.

In addition to actual financial arrangements, the Playbook can contain a list of last wishes or requests for your last remains. For example, you might desire to have a certain song played at a memorial or a favorite flower present. You might want to make sure that your memorial is more of a celebration than a funeral. All of these things can be written in a simple letter or word document and put in your Playbook.

A Playbook pioneer shared a thoughtful idea of leaving love letters to those who are left behind. We discussed the benefits of telling people how you feel about them while you are alive being very important, but the idea of leaving a letter echoing that, might be meaningful to a lot of people during such a time as the losing of a loved one.

Legal Contracts and Employment Contracts

Not everyone has contract relationships with other parties; in fact, I'd say that most of us don't. But if you do keep a copy of your contract in your Playbook. Contracts can be for employment or obligations from one party to another. Remember that the Playbook is part of your organizational system to keep track of all of your affairs. Additionally, it's your system to manage your affairs. Contracts can be a significant part of cash flow or future cash flow and are certainly something you want to track.

One Playbook Pioneer would often make private loans to friends and acquaintances. Usually not a good idea, despite the relatively high-interest rates the pioneer could charge, because the default risk can be high and eventually was a reality. Before the Playbook, the loan contracts were often hard to find and not understood by anyone other than the pioneer.

After our pioneer placed the contracts in the Playbook, it was easier to review this information with advisors as well as with family members who might be impacted by the loans. When a default did occur, the team of advisors who all had a familiarity with the

Playbook were able to communicate much more effectively in mitigating the losses.

The Playbook can serve as a starting point for trusted advisors to locate the resources needed to assist with a problem.

Property Registration Records, Like Transfer on Death and Trust Registrations

So, imagine you got this very detailed trust work done. You found that some of your most important goals could be accomplished by reregistering your assets to include beneficiaries. You invested countless hours carefully going through your NWS to make sure all your assets are included in your plan. Finally, you have spent thousands of dollars hiring a great legal team to make sure everything was addressed. Wow, what a relief to get all that done. And, at least for now, you are pretty sure you or your team did a thorough job.

But then a year later your spouse says, "Are we sure that all of our assets are correctly titled because I just heard about a couple that missed a few things and it caused a lot of problems"? You stare at your spouse blankly for a second. You are pretty sure you did a complete and diligent job, but that was a year ago. Did the county record the property the way it was supposed to? Did everything get taken care of as it should have? Oh man, the only way to be sure is to go to the county and double-check the property registration to make sure it got filed correctly. You realize your Monday now includes a trip to the county records department.

Then imagine that you went to the trouble of recording the new registration of the property at the county and you got a copy of the transaction from the county that is now filed in your Playbook. When your spouse asks about the titling of property, you confidently look your spouse in the eye and say, "We can double-check the Playbook. That's why we have it". Or better yet, your spouse doesn't even bother to ask you about the titling of property because checking the Playbook is now on the spouse's list because your spouse knows the program. You have learned your lesson well—always get a receipt!

The Beneficiary Review Form

Many people have one or perhaps two pieces of real estate and potentially dozens of accounts like IRAs, checking accounts, ROTH IRAs, stock accounts, 401ks, etc. etc. Additionally, many of us should keep track of insurance policies and the listed beneficiaries. With sometimes dozens of accounts to be kept track of for beneficiaries, we've found that a beneficiary review form is a great way to document that you have double checked the beneficiary designations on all listed accounts. When the need or concern arises, you can review the beneficiary review form and see your work.

I'd suggest that on each account or asset you have, list the following:

- Who is/are the primary beneficiary or beneficiaries?
- Who is/are the contingent beneficiary or beneficiaries?
- What percentage goes to each listed beneficiary?

- Are the beneficiaries per stirpes or ProRata? (see note below)
- What is the date that this information was verified?

A Beneficiary Summary might look something like this:

April 1st 2020			
Account #	Description	Primary	Contingent
1234-2233	Johns IRA at LPL	Jill 100%	Jane (50%) Jack (50%) **Per stirpes**
3241-1111	Jill's Life Insurance State Farm	John 100%	Jane (50%) Jack (50%) **Per stirpes**

A few key terms are going to be helpful to understand. How your beneficiaries are designated can be important. Let's take a look at the difference between per stirpes and Prorata.

Per stirpes: This designation on beneficiaries means that if the beneficiary is no longer living, then his or her share will pass down to his or her estate. Put another way, it will go to the beneficiary of the beneficiary. We see this request often when parents leave assets to their children. If one of the children dies before the parents, this type of beneficiary designation will assist with the grandchildren or surviving spouse in receiving those assets.

Prorata: This designations on beneficiaries mean that if the beneficiary is no longer living, then his or her share will be split up among the remaining beneficiaries already named. For example: if three beneficiaries are getting a third each, but one had passed away, the remaining two beneficiaries would now get half each. We see this often when parents have children but no grandchildren.

Most companies will default to 'Prorata.' It's much easier for a financial institution to divide remaining assets between those who survive rather than tracking down the heirs of the deceased beneficiaries. The time and effort it can take to research and prove who now gets the assets can be costly. In fact, it's often a matter of probate. If it's left up to financial institutions, they will make things easier. However, this might not be what you want. Double-check to find out what type of designation your beneficiaries have; it's important.

The Schedule A –
Personal Property Disposition List

You might see it by another name, but the Schedule A is simply a list of personal property and instructions on how to distribute that property at death. These Schedule A's are often overlooked or just left blank.

While many important things pass to heirs by title and will be controlled by beneficiary designations or court order (probate), some things don't for example, pieces of art. Typically, no title exists on such things. Jewelry, collectibles, appliances, clothes, furniture, antiques, guns, personal memorabilia; all of these things tend to 'grow legs and walk away'. For these things, if we want them to go where we'd like, a Schedule A is helpful. It's then up to the executor to get them into the right hands but at least she knows your wishes.

Having a documented list of where things go may:

1. create less havoc and fighting among heirs

2. create documentation in the event a legal issue comes up, and

3. allow you to keep an inventory of meaningful and potentially valuable things

A List of Not So Obvious
People, Places and Things

Finally, the Estate and Legal Document section of your Playbook can contain a lot of useful information that will help not only during your life but after your life. That information is going to assist your heirs in wrapping things up for you or continuing your legacy. As with the personal property disposition list mentioned above, you may want to provide instructions for a few additional things. The following is a list of examples you might include with notes in your Playbook to remind, assist, or ease the efforts of those picking up the pieces:

- Special people to get in touch with that could help with arrangements or should be invited to arrangements.
- Special people to share stories or memories.
- Places you might have stored things like storage units, safe deposit boxes.

- Hiding spots around the house folded up 20-dollar bills in the suit pockets.
- Where you keep your journal.
- A list of social media accounts to notify.

How the Estate Planning and Legal Documents Section of the Playbook Ties into the Rest of the Book

- **The Goals and Objectives section** of the Playbook might indicate specific goals for what happens with your estate plan. For many people, goals not only include during life goals but post-life goals as well. For example, we might have a goal to fund a charitable bequest when we pass.

- **The Financial Statements section**, particularly the Net Worth Statement, is going to be instrumental in preparing your estate plan. Having an understanding of your Net Worth and what type of assets you have will impact what type of estate planning you are going to do.

- **The Insurance section** of your Playbook might contain estate planning strategies like a last to die policy, and because the life insurance proceeds are included in your gross estate, your estate plan needs to be aware of such policies.

- **The Tax section** of your Playbook may assist with the last return that someone will have prepared on your behalf the estate return. This section often keeps track of gifts that might offset the unified credit, tax information regarding charitable planning, and general documentation that will assist with estate planning.

- **The Social Security and Pension section** of your Playbook might contain information about survivor benefits that are important or period certain guarantees on payouts. For example, if your social security payments are higher than your spouses, your spouse will likely be able to get the higher of the two at your death if you pass first. Additionally, if you have elected lifetime income on a pension, that election may have included benefits that last for a period actually exceeding your life.

- **The Performance Reporting section** of the Playbook can often indicate how much we are going to need estate planning. If our assets keep growing beyond our ability to keep up with that growth or to use the principal, we better take a really good look at how we plan on leaving those assets behind.

From the Playbook Players

Various Colored Stickers Method

A now Playbook Pioneer used to have stickers of various colors put on the back of all of her personal belongings at her house. The system assigned a color to all the kids, and the idea was simply that the kids would sort through the items and take them home according to the stickers.

One day, the Playbook Pioneer found one daughter replacing some stickers with her own color! When converting over to the Schedule A system, the problem of outside influences was greatly reduced.

Assumption of What Is Meaningful

Another Playbook Pioneer taught me the importance of having a meaningful conversation with your beneficiaries about what they would want rather than *assuming* they would want certain items.

For example, the pocketknife your grandfather carried around, or the paintbrush set your grandmother uses might be of much greater importance to you than anything else. If your grandkids or kids told you how important an item was to them, you could give it to them now or make sure it's recorded on your Schedule A. After all, grandpa might still be using that knife, and grandma isn't planning on giving up the easel just yet.

Not Dotting All the I's and Missing One Account Registration

While everything went according to plan when it came to the distribution of assets, one account left unchecked caused some problems.

When grandpa passed away, he had a small IRA account at a bank. It was worth around $2000.00. The primary beneficiary on the account was grandma. But grandma had already passed away. When the kids went to inquire about the IRA account, they found out that the beneficiary designations never got updated when grandma passed. The bank then told them that the secondary beneficiary was listed as the estate. As a result of listing the estate as a secondary beneficiary, it was subject to probate. But first, the family had to track down grandmas' death certificate to prove she wasn't alive.

Not only did the family struggle to come up with grandmas' death certificate, but they ended up just ignoring the money at the bank because the $2000.00 split five ways just wasn't worth anyone pursuing it by themselves. No one was talking to each other at the time.

I recommend never listing the estate as a beneficiary of any type. It goes against the very reason for listing a beneficiary. It is, in fact, the default for not listing any beneficiary. If you take an exam and put down the wrong answer for every question, you will get an F. This is the same thing as leaving every question blank with no answer; it's still an F, but at least you saved the ink. Either way, please don't list the estate as a beneficiary and don't leave the beneficiary designation blank either.

Why the Beneficiary Review Is Important

Somehow between the birth of my twin boys and the birth of my third son two and a half years later, I got so busy with life I didn't update several of my beneficiary designations until my youngest son was four years old. Life got so busy that I forgot to deal with it.

I've been practicing financial management and planning for decades, but I was, at least in this instance, the classic example of the shoe cobbler! Having a method to review information like beneficiary designations is important because it can be easy to forget to make updates when life is busy.

CHAPTER FOUR

Insurance Coverage

Insurance can be one of those funny areas of bill paying that leaves us potentially feeling frustrated. We shrug our shoulders, shake our heads and pay the premium even though we know we may never get a return of that money; in fact, we hope we don't.

We write that check or pay that auto premium periodically to pass on the risk of us experiencing a loss, to someone else, the insurance company. If we experience that loss, the word indemnification comes to mind. Loosely defined, it means to make whole again after a loss. That's what insurance is supposed to do for us; make up for a loss. But, regardless of indemnification, none of us rational-minded people not prone to fraud would want to experience the loss regardless of whether we have insurance.

In some cases insurance is required and in some cases, it's optional. That gives us all something in common and also gives us the ability to make choices for ourselves. Given that we have required insurance, we will all need to track and deal with our insurance coverage. That's where the Playbook comes in.

In this section we will deal with:

- The Insurance Summary Sheet
- What you need to save and what you don't
- The Price vs. The Value of Insurance
- The continuum of self-insured vs. fully insured
- Different types of insurance for you to consider and understand
- Making sure you have the coverage you need, or you think you have

Before jumping in and tackling our list above, I add this disclosure; insurance transfers risk from one party to another. It can be a complicated mess, partly due to the highly regulated industry, and our legal system. The ever changing landscape of requirements and scope of insurance is daunting.

I have a tremendous amount of respect for insurance professionals and their ability to pull all the pieces together on behalf of their clients. If you have the choice to go at it alone in management of your insurance and choose to do so, I hope you find this chapter helpful. But, I don't believe this or any other volume of work you might find will come close to generating the understanding that can be provided by a dedicated professional.

Now, onto something easy, helpful and impactful.

The Insurance Summary Sheet

In the very first page of the insurance section of your Playbook, you may want to put a one page summary of your insurance policies. We don't need the details here, but rather a simple list that includes the policy number, the insurance company, and a brief description of the policy. Think of this as the 50,000 ft view of your coverage. You may need quick access to the policy numbers and it is helpful for your heirs and helpers to have a summary of what you've got going on.

Your summary page might look something like the example below:

Policy Number	Insurance Co.	Description
12-2312-BX	Safe Ins. Co	Motorcycle Insurance on Yamaha
2555-555BB	Everystate Co.	Auto on Ford Truck
P100Dludi222	Telnet Ins. Co.	Auto on Telsa
5444.22	Safe Ins. Co.	Home insurance 515 Nie St.
LF444333	Everystate Co.	Life policy on Jack - whole life
LF443444	Everystate Co.	D.I. Policy on Diane
FHP4011PY	Model H.I. Co.	Group Family Health Plan

I don't believe you need to add too many details here. Just simply having the policy numbers helps to make sure you are not duplicating your efforts. For example, I've got several life policies that look identical but are, in fact, different. Since the policy numbers are all unique, keeping track of them by policy number ensures that I don't either ignore a policy or forget it because I think I've already listed it.

Listing the insurance company is an easy way to identify what statement I might need if I want more information. The description is nothing more than a memory jogger for me and a quick look for my advisors.

What You Need to Save and What You Don't

As with many other areas of your financial life, insurance seems to generate massive amounts of mail. Even opting to go paperless doesn't seem to completely stop the mailbox from overflowing with notifications, disclosures, advertising, and what the heck are privacy notices. And of course, if you do opt to go paperless, the one thing that you really need, an actual statement, might not come at all. So, let's talk about what is important to save and what isn't. Remember, in your Playbook, it's all about keeping what is meaningful so you can narrow your focus and getting rid of all the clutter that doesn't have meaning.

After two decades of financial planning experience, I have a good understanding of those insurance papers that come in the mail. Part of the scope of financial planning is insurance coverage and review. However, it wasn't until I reached out to several insurance professionals who have practiced equally as long as I have in my *own* field, and after spending countless hours of research on the subject with Playbook Pioneers and equal amounts of time scouring the internet that I can proudly say the following. There is no right or wrong answer, only a few good suggestions. Boy, what a letdown!

A Few Good Suggestions

<u>Keep your Declaration pages</u>. A Declaration page is the document that comes once a year or once every six months that states what your coverage amounts to moving forward. It's typically 1-4 pages long and contains most of the details you would ever need to know in determining what types of benefits you have or to be able to communicate to an insurance professional what types of insurance you have. These are very common for coverage like property insurance, auto insurance, workers' compensation, renters' insurance, and any other type of insurance that is continuously evolving in terms of the price and coverage.

Just like with your financial statements, you don't need to keep all the records for the same policy. For example, don't keep the old declaration pages for the same automobile. You could keep the records for all the coverage you have on the same asset to track the cost and coverage differences over the years, but what good would it do? If you are concerned with price, shop your coverage around periodically. But to track it from period to period is just going to be an ugly reminder of the inflation that exists. What you might be better off doing is replacing the old Declaration page with the new one and making a quick note of the difference. Better to one touch the change than to create a system for tracking the differences. The past is the past. Keep your headlights brighter than your taillights.

Keep your Benefit Summary Page. If you are lucky, your health insurance, dental insurance, vision insurance, long-term care insurance, or disability insurance, will provide you with a one or two page summary of your benefits at each policy renewal. This summary is a great thing to store. That way, you'll have easy access to a list of what your coverages you have in an easy to read format. Just like the Declaration pages for assets, you can replace the Benefit Summary page each time you get a new one. Same argument, let the past be the past, focus on what you have.

If you want to create a history of your insurance premiums over the last decade, that's a book you are going to write. Not a filing system that will eventually confuse you or the unfortunate loved one to pick up the pieces.

Keep copies of ID cards. Most of us carry our ID cards around with us in the event we need them. I use an app on my phone to store my ID cards, so I don't have to carry a copy. I do have a few benefit providers who act frustrated when I can't produce the card for them to scan. Then they either have to get an email copy or read it off my phone, but hey we're moving to a paperless world.

So instead, I keep copies or the original cards in my Playbook. That way, I've got them just in case I run into that really tough medical records person who insists on the original card. I don't really think that is going to happen though. More likely, I'll drop my phone in the water and not have a backup available and so the actual cards will be nice to have.

Keep annual statements from life insurance. If you have life insurance, and depending on what type, you probably get a statement every so often. Keep at least one statement for each policy. The most recent one if possible. They come out infrequently enough that you won't be running to your Playbook that often to update statements.

I get several statements each year for various policies. Just like the other statements, I remove and shred the old ones and replace them with the newest statements. If the policy happens to be more of an investment than a life insurance policy such as a highly funded variable universal life insurance policy sold with the premise of being a supplemental retirement source, you might consider keeping this in the Financial Statements section of the playbook. If it's Term Life Insurance, it probably belongs here in the Insurance Coverage section.

Keep any special coverage or temporary insurance documents. If you happen to get some coverage for a trip, for example, you can keep the information here and clean it out on your next Playbook review after your trip. If you happen to have a special policy for anything not already covered, keep it here. Having insurance comes down to keeping track of and understanding what you have, and then, hoping you don't have to use it.

Do not keep insurance binders or policies. What? That sounds like insane advice. It's a contract, right? You could put that big old binder or policy in your safe deposit box. You will never need it, but if you feel the need to keep it, do so. The insurance company will keep a copy of the policy on file, and pertinent details are all on the summary page or declaration page or annual statement that you get anyway. The fine print if you really must have access to it can be reissued by the company. If that in anyway makes you feel uncomfortable, keep it. But, put it away someplace safe and if you happen to get rid of the policy make sure you get rid of the binder.

<u>Do not keep newsletters or company financial statements</u>. By company financial statements in this case I am talking about earning reports *for* the company. These items are one touch or no touch. Look at them, and If they add value, share them or make notes, but you don't need to keep them. They certainly don't belong in your playbook. Financial statements of this nature are available online and company newsletters are not that exciting.

Part of the Playbook process is to focus on what is essential and minimize distractions that are not important. Getting your financial life into one binder is possible and probable if you follow this path, but you can't be a packrat of non-impactful paperwork.

<u>Do not keep annual privacy notice requirements.</u> What the heck are these privacy notices anyway?... Under the Gramm-Leach-Bliley Act, financial institutions are required to provide an annual disclosure of their privacy policies to their customers. Insert fitting emoji here that express my frustration with a law that produces such a waste of resources. If you really must read one of these to feel diligent, then please do so. If you would like my permission to dispose of such nonsense, permission granted.

The Price vs. Value of Insurance

I think part of the reason that the price we pay for insurance can often bother us so much is because we don't see the value in it until we experience a loss. Then, hopefully the insurance covers our loss. Even then, we may have paid more into the insurance than we receive out of it. And while the price for the insurance everything else being equal can be the same, it's the value of insurance that will vary a great deal among consumers.

Price is clear, it's the dollars we layout to purchase a policy. Value is what we get out of a policy. Value varies. One value might be the actual coverage of a loss. If the loss is large, the value would be different than if the loss as small. Another value is peace of mind. Let's face it, knowing that you have a base level of wealth, in part because it's protected against unforeseen loss, allows us to keep our focus on more productive areas. There is also a certain value that exists for your credit rating. Yes, if you are not potentially on the hook for a fire burning down your house, you are less of a credit risk.

While the idea that your credit risk is less if you carry insurance might be more theoretical than practical, the idea that I can rely on someone to perform more consistently because they have transferred risk to another party is valid. For example, I'm more likely to hire a nanny who has health insurance than one that does not. Everything else being equal, I'd rather rely on the nanny who is less likely to be sick because of preventative illness programs available and access to modern practices, than rely on a nanny who might plan to cross that bridge when they get to it. The latter nanny has me concerned about an illness getting out of hand and leaving me high and dry for childcare.

The value of insurance is certainly subjective. Depending on what is important to the consumer, one policy might be of much greater value to one person than to another. I might have a strong need for a policy covering the unlimited tech help offered when purchasing a new computer because of my self-admitted incompetence with computer issues. So, I place a great deal of value on the policy. Another person might be so competent with their own abilities that they would not value such a policy at all. Even though the policy would be sold to both of us for the same price, because I value the policy more it is worth more to me.

For many types of insurance policies, there are deductibles, waiting periods, elimination periods, maximum benefits, maximum out of pocket expenses, inclusions, exclusions, the list goes on and on. Each of these variables can have a different value to different consumers. In reality, there are thousands and thousands of different combinations of variables that will affect price and the value of a policy. The point we might understand from this is that to compare the cost of insurance, we have to look at the variables to understand what we are getting. To understand the value of the variables, we had better know our own preferences for our insurance. Do you want to be fully insured or self-insured to the extent possible? That's a good place to start.

The Continuum of Self Insured vs. Fully Insured

Imagine a line or continuum with two sides. On one side of the continuum, you have the person who does not want insurance at all, wishes to keep the risk of loss themselves and as a result not have to pay insurance premiums. This concept is known as self-insurance or risk retention. If someone can completely eliminate the risk, the concept is known as risk avoidance. In the event the risk can be reduced, risk reduction. The idea of insurance is, of course, risk transfer.

Sadly though, many of these strategies come at a cost but they also can add value. Let's say that I'm offered an insurance policy on a new computer I buy. If I pay an extra $50.00, I'd have an extended warranty that lasts an additional two years. If I'm wanting to self-insure, I'd decline the extended warranty and retain the risk of computer failure after the standard warranty myself.

On the other side of the continuum, we've got the person who wants to transfer all the risk and not bear any themselves. This person will elect full coverage on vehicles, have the lowest deductible possible, and always buy the extended warranties when available. Nothing wrong with this strategy. The argument would be that the owner of the policy has peace of mind that they value more than the person declining the offer. Or, perhaps they believe the insurance would be particularly important for them.

Somewhere in the middle of the continuum is the person who recognizes that transferring the risk for some things like home insurance is something they would certainly take advantage of, but they might opt-out on other things like extended warranties. This person perhaps doesn't like insurance but also recognizes that some risk is just worth transferring to others.

To understand where we fall on the continuum, it is important for us and our advisors to consider different options, levels, and or amounts of insurance. Knowing that we have or someone else has a strong bias towards getting rid of risk is going to be important in discussing the optimal amount of insurance. Knowing that we or someone else has a strong bias towards no insurance, is going to lead to choices of risk reduction, retention or elimination.

And of course, the idea of the risk continuum is not two dimensional. If it were only that easy to discover where we landed on the risk continuum, we could make all insurance decisions in the future based on that. The reality is that as we have different areas of our lives that have different plots along the continuum. For example, I might be more than happy to pass on the extended warranty of the new computer, but I might buy the travel insurance every time.

As we discuss a few different types of insurance below with some general comments—you may get a sense for my own biases and preferences. Hopefully when it comes to your decisions, you will be able to identify your own preferences.

Different Types of Insurance for You to Consider and Be Familiar with

In this section, I'll cover what to keep for various types of insurance, a brief description of each type, and in some cases a bit of general advice on the various types of insurance mentioned.

Health Insurance: For tracking purposes, professionals in that arena recommend you keep a copy of your insurance card as well as a Benefits Summary page. Accomplished Playbook Pioneers keep what is important and get rid of what is not. Cleary health insurance covers things like trips to the doctor and cost of major health issue. But, did you know that many insurance plans also encourage members to have gym memberships by offering a discount? Given that someone's health is so very important, and a lot of emotional issues are present, having some really good advice on health care is worthwhile.

Disability insurance: For tracking purposes, just like with health insurance, you should keep a copy of your Benefits Summary page. Often with Disability, things like waiting period, maximum benefit, elimination periods, can vary by policy to a great degree. Knowing in a quick summary what you have is ideal for tracking and making good decisions.

Disability Insurance covers you for lost work when you can't perform certain functions like getting dressed. Often a doctor will have to attest that you are disabled. This type of insurance is not meant to have a benefit period that lasts too long. Usually, around one year and after that point, most people would rely on Social Security disability.

Social Security disability typically has the strictest standards to qualify for benefits, and many disability policies will pay out where Social Security might not.

Disability insurance is one type of policy that I'd recommend for someone who needs to rely on his or her income to avoid large financial setbacks. If you have to work to pay your mortgage, you might consider disability. If you have built up savings, or if you have a positive and ever-growing net worth, you might consider 'self-insuring' on this one. Save the premiums, add them to your investments, and take care of it yourself. If you have an incident and can't work, just make sure you have access to funds to pay bills and live.

Umbrella policy: For tracking, you need to hang onto the declaration page for this policy. It contains all of the relevant information you need to review your coverage in the event you need it, or you want to assess its value given the cost.

An Umbrella policy is really for someone who has a positive net worth or plenty of potential to have positive net worth. It covers you typically in a lawsuit where another party is suing you for your assets, or soon to be assets. This policy is going to go above and beyond the limits in a homeowners or automobile coverage. For example, you might have a $500,000.00 per incident limit on your automobile coverage, but if you have run into a Lamborghini full of kids who all require extensive emotional counseling to the tune of millions, you might be in trouble. That's where the umbrella policy kicks in.

Do we really live in such a litigious world that this is a possibility? Yes, we do. The cost of umbrella policies is really low, and something I'd recommend if you either have assets or have the ability to have assets. If you don't have assets or the ability to get them well then you are not much of a target for a lawsuit. You might be better off skipping the umbrella policy.

Life Insurance: Get ready for a polarized conversation. First, when it comes to life insurance, hang onto your policy declaration pages you get each year.

There are generally two types of policies available with many variations of each. In general, there are term policies and whole life policies. Term policies last as long as the term of the insurance. For example, a 10-year term would provide insurance for ten years, and then on the 11th year, the policy would expire; no more insurance. Usually the policy doesn't expire, but the cost of insurance goes up so much that generally, you will not want to pay it. Term insurance is typically the lowest cost insurance where you are just transferring the risk of premature death to an insurance provider and only paying for that.

Whole Life policies are intended to last as long as you last but often will mature at a certain age like 100. The policy maturing means the death benefit is paid out at that time, even if you are still alive. It loses its tax benefit at that point, and what you get back isn't a death benefit as much as a return of what you paid into the policy with potentially some earnings. Whole life policies will typically have a defined outcome in terms of the policy performance ahead of time not a lot of guessing on what will happen other than the life expectancy of the insured.

A subgroup of policies exists within this category that have no certain outcomes to speak of. Universal life and variable universal life policies were popular alternatives to tax-free savings at one point before Roth IRAs. These policies provide a separate account where a portion of the premiums, above and beyond the cost of insurance, that keeps going up every year by the way, will be invested. If the investments do well, you could benefit greatly. If they don't, you might either surrender the policy or might have to dump more money than you expected into it to keep it afloat.

Advice from the trenches: I've seen whole life policies and variations written over the years, and I've seen very little evidence to support the idea that the client met his or her expectation from policy. Granted, we've been in a very volatile stock market where a lot of assumptions ahead of time have been tested. However, the idea of owning life insurance is certainly worthy of consideration. I'd rather pay the lowest cost and have the coverage for only as long as I need it. Buy term. Save money and invest. As much as I'd like to believe it, life insurance, no matter how it is diced up, doesn't seem to be a good investment it's not supposed to; it's only supposed to transfer risk.

Do you need life insurance at all? If you have a net worth built up that combined with other potential benefits assist those that rely on you when you are gone, such as social security survivor benefits, with living out the lives you would hope for them financially, you might not need life insurance. At some point, you are hopefully wealthy enough that if you pass away, the survivors in your financial wake will be just fine. However, if you are in a position where your loved ones or dependents wouldn't survive in the way you or they would wish, you should consider carrying life insurance.

Life insurance covers the risk of you dying early. It shouldn't be purchased to cover the risk of you dying. Dying happens no matter what and isn't a risk; it's a fact.

Here are a few additional reasons that life insurance can be useful:

1. Liquidity for estate dissolution – if most of the assets are tied up, but the heirs are going to need some cold hard cash to pay taxes or other expenses, and they don't want to or can't sell the assets.

2. <u>Divorce decrees</u> – one party is responsible for spousal support or another arrangement, and life insurance might be a solution for ensuring that the payments could continue at the death of that party.

3. <u>Contractual obligations</u> – sometimes like divorce decrees, the death of one party might impact the business outcome of another party.

4. <u>Key Person Insurance</u> – often a solution for a business that would be negatively impacted by the loss of a critical partner or employee.

5. <u>Buy/Sell agreements</u> – insurance can provide needed funds for one party to purchase another parties interest in a business or asset if one party passes prematurely.

<u>Auto/RV/motorcycle insurance</u>: Here, the annual or semiannual policy declarations are all you need to keep. However, you might consider saving your ID cards or a copy in your Playbook, as well. Unlike your Health Insurance ID cards that will typically only change when you change providers, these insurances cards will change at every renewal.

Making Sure You Have the Coverage You Need, or You Think You Have

Having the right amount of insurance in place is important. Since insurance isn't typically sold down to the penny, it's nearly impossible to get the exact correct amount. It's also very subjective, and you have personal biases that will place your ideal amount at some point along the continuum, while others will be better served with a different amount. Further, consultants, advisors and other professionals come with their own biases. But they are also trained to help you identify and prioritize your preferences.

There are, however, certainly examples of wrong amounts. I'll share two quick stories of people I know, and insurance coverage that they had, which proved to be, in one way or another, the wrong coverage in the From the Playbook Players Section.

How the Insurance Section of the Playbook Ties into the Rest of the Book

- In **the Goals and Objectives section**, you may spend time articulating your preferences for insurance coverage. The insurance section should be a reflection of your preferences. You might also have goals that you want to insure happen because they are so important to you. For example, a common goal for young families is to make sure the surviving spouse and children would be cared for if a premature death occurred.

- In **the Financial Statements section** of the Playbook, your Net Worth Statement is going to indicate where your assets are and where your risk is. That's an important insurance consideration. If you have all of your assets in one spot you'd better have insurance on that spot. Your Cash Flow Statement might indicate where your monetary obligations are and help you identify what would be a problem for you if some of the income went away.

- In **the Estate and Legal Documents section**, you might have goals like bequest motives requiring liquidity at the death of a stakeholder. Or, you might need to think about compensating a custodian or guardian if you are doing some planning for minor children.

- In **the Tax section** of the Playbook, you may find that some insurance premiums qualify for special tax treatment that you will need to bring to the attention of your tax preparer.

- In the **Social Security and Pension section**, you might elect to take a straight life pension payout, which has no remaining amount for a surviving spouse. That might be a good need or use for life insurance.

- In **the Performance section** of the Playbook, you might consider what happens to your plans if you don't get the performance you are expecting. Did you know you can insure performance as well?

From the Playbook Players

Too Little Insurance

A friend and client of mine I've known for years had a fire burn down an outbuilding he owned. His building was a three-bay garage, one being for an RV, which was detached from the primary residence and finished extremely well. It was the envy of most guys with toys. It was, of course fully insulated and finished not only with sheetrock but was painted on the inside with molding and trim everywhere the eye could see. It looked more like a living space than a garage. And what living space would be complete without a kitchen and a bathroom. Well, this one wouldn't, and it wasn't. It was a fine outbuilding!

This outbuilding was so fine that in the process of the owner taking out a loan to purchase the home, the outbuilding was assigned a value somewhere in the neighborhood of $130k. The appraiser who came to assess the house when a mortgage was taken out was certainly impressed. The underwriters for the mortgage company based the loan off a value of the home plus the value of the outbuilding. From the underwriter's perspective, they were loaning money with a lien on property worth the home value plus the outbuilding value of 130k. A lien for an underwriter is what makes the loan possible. If the asset the lien is on is worth less, the loan can't be for as much. A clear relationship exists between the value of the property and the potential loan.

When the insurance provider created insurance coverage on the property, the insurance provider allowed only $60k worth of coverage for the outbuilding. When the insurance was written, the cost to replace a 3-bay garage as an outbuilding was $60k. The insurance agent and underwriters of the policy didn't bother to peer into the garage to see that it was finished in a manner that it would require $130k to rebuild. Why the mortgage company holding the loan didn't review the insurance documents I don't know.

So, when the fire took place, the outbuilding was a total loss. Fortunately, besides some personal property, that was the only loss. Once the smoke settled, my friend called his insurance agent, and the insurance agent made quick work of paying the claim. My friend received the check for $60k but noticed something strange. The check was made payable to not only him but the mortgage company as well. And that makes sense; after all, they had a lien on the property. My friend then contacted the mortgage company who broke this bit of shocking news to him. He was going to be required to bring the building back up to pre-loss condition before the mortgage company would assist in cashing the check.

From their perspective, they loaned my friend money to buy the house along with the outbuilding and didn't want to end up with an outbuilding that cost only $60k to rebuild when they loaned money based on a building worth $130k. It made sense. As you can imagine, this created all sorts of stress and anxiety for not only my friend but the insurance company and other parties.

My friend ended up refinancing based on a different loan amount with a different mortgage company before the check was finally reissued. This cost time, money and caused a lot of headaches.

What does this story illustrate? Well, for one, you better make sure that if you have an asset you are insuring for replacement value, you actually have the right amount of insurance. My friend got away with paying a lesser premium each year, but in the end, he didn't have the coverage he thought he did. That might have been discovered with a good review of the policy he got originally or if his agent had done a little more work ahead of time to determine the right amount of coverage needed. Regardless of how it happened, it did.

Know your coverage. Know your values. Having the wrong amount of insurance can not only leave you exposed for losses beyond your insurance, it can create cost beyond the losses if you have to make accommodations to satisfy other parties, like a lender.

Too Much Insurance or Insurance Not Needed

A colleague of mine told me a story that had impacted his family quite negatively. This is a story about buying a life insurance policy on the patriarch of the family who lived a lot longer than anticipated.

In this case, the family was reunited with the patriarch about 15 years before his death when he was in his late 70's. With a multiple pack of cigarettes per day habit and other signs of poor health, the family thought it might be a profitable venture to purchase some life insurance on the patriarch who willingly agreed because it wasn't his money after all.

If you have any idea of how life insurance works, then you can image how expensive the policy was to buy. Old age + smoker = high premiums. Each month the family had to fork over a large amount of money to the life insurance company to continue the whole life policy. The premiums, what the consumer would pay, on this particular policy start small but grew every year. Eventually, the family was splitting up the cost among itself to afford the 1200.00 a month it had to pay to keep the policy in force. By the 15ᵗʰ year, they had put so much money into the policy that they didn't feel like they could afford to drop it.

The colleague was approached by the family two years before the patriarch's death. At that point, he tried to persuade the family to stop paying altogether because if the patriarch lived longer than two years, the death benefits from the life insurance policy would be worth less than what they were going to have to pay over the next two years. The money they had already spent was just gone, a sunk cost.

Two years later, the policy did payout. At that point, it was unclear exactly how much was put into the policy, but we know that the last two years amounted to about what the policy paid out. The first thirteen years were never recovered. This was a clear example of a bad use of insurance.

A Few Lessons from the Patriarch's Life Insurance Story

1. Regardless of whether or not an insurable interest exists so you can buy insurance, you really shouldn't buy insurance if you don't need it. We as consumers are not smarter than the insurance industry. If you hold some sort of well kept secret that you are not telling the insurance company when the underwriting occurs, that's called fraud.

2. As previously mentioned, don't buy a whole life policy. Buy a term policy and keep it in force as long as you need it and then let it expire. Don't be caught in the trap of paying more and more premiums every year to support a policy you probably don't need. If you happen to be one of the rare people who can clearly justify why you need a whole life policy, be sure you know what you are getting into.

3. The Sunk Cost Fallacy comes to mind here, doesn't it? Continue a behavior or endeavor as a result of previously invested resources even though you know it's a bad idea. You can't afford to stop. Also known as sunk cost bias. This is why I argue to buy term. If the asset or life exist longer than the term, you don't lose, you win!

CHAPTER FIVE

Tax Preparation and Storage

While death and taxes are said to be the only certainties in life, please do not be afraid of this section! The tax reporting area is meant to make that annual event of filing a return easier, as well as giving you access to the information that will enable your team of advisors to *play* their best for you. No promises here, but it's possible you might look forward to tax time once you start utilizing your Playbook.

For most people, the Playbook can contain everything you need to save for your tax preparations and short-term storage. The Playbook is going to contain what is essential for preparing your taxes each year, and what is often needed by your service providers to assist you with making long term decisions or taking some immediate action. In addition to the Playbook, you may need to have a long-term storage where you keep your older returns. We'll get into why you might need to keep those returns a little later.

For those of you who might own and operate several businesses or have complicated corporate returns, you might find that housing all of your information in the Playbook is a challenge. Not only are your returns complex and potentially massive in size, but you have several schedules and supporting documentation that are too cumbersome to fit into the Playbook. You may not only need a long term storage solution for your returns, but you may also need a separate filing system for your tax preparation efforts.

Even if you are someone who falls in the camp of being too complex for exclusive use of the Playbook for tax reporting, you are still going to find that it serves a great purpose for your household. Apply and adopt as much as you can and modify where you can't. I'm amazed at all that I can organize within my playbook, even if I must create other files to assist with more complicated arrangements. It's not duplicative, and what I do in my Playbook in this section, enhances other sections of my Playbook.

In this section of the Playbook, we will cover:

- Storing documents for tax preparation
- Keeping your tax returns
- Storing necessary long term items
- What not to store.

Let's dive in.

Storing Documents for Tax Preparation

Throughout the year, you will be collecting a few things along the way that you are going to need at tax time. You either have a filing cabinet, digital or physical, that you store information in for tax preparation or you put them in a drawer or glove box of your car. I've actually had people tell me they do this. Whatever the method is, you can easily replace the process with the Playbook. I find that most things can be three-hole punched and stored in my Playbook rather easily. In the event I don't want to three-hole punch for some reason then I'll just use a sheet protector. Either way, anything that I get throughout the year that I need at tax time goes in my playbook.

A few examples:

- Property tax statements they come out in October: After I double-check them and pay them if need be, I three-hole punch them, and in my Playbook they go.

- 5498's: These guys come out in May and are my copy of what I contributed to my retirement accounts during the previous year. Note: they come out after the filing deadline, so most people have their taxes done when they receive them. I store them in my Playbook, and I have them for my next trip to my tax advisor.

- Charitable contribution receipts: Many of these come out after the first of the year and come in the mail. However, when I make a cash or in-kind donation, I may receive the receipt at that time. Either way, I'm not going to want to lose these valuable potential deductions.

- W2's: These are usually mailed by the end of January or early February. This handy little reporting item is important if you have employment somewhere and are getting a paycheck.

- 1099's and K1's: These forms come in many different varieties. But, they all report either an income or expense that is going to have an impact on your taxes. Again, look for them in January or February but you may get these in March or even April.

Most people will have some system in place for dealing with storing documents for taxes. What I really like about having it inside your Playbook is that, along with your tax returns for several years, all of the other sections of your playbook greatly enhance the ability of your advisors to guide you into good decisions holistically. Or, if you self-advise, you have everything at your fingertips for your own analysis.

Keeping Your Tax Returns

Why keep your tax returns? After all, we live in a digital age, and the IRS knows what you've filed. Why should you keep a copy? Let's deal with the obvious:

1. You often must show your tax returns. This has been a hot topic on many fronts for things like loans or to apply for aid.

2. Your tax returns are a record of what happened during the year financially. You might have to draw upon that record at some point to prove what happened.

3. You might get an audit someday and want to have a copy of what you filed along with supporting documents so you can defend your filing.

So, with your tax returns, you are going to break down the storage into two parts. The first part is going to be for your Playbook. The second part is going to be for your long term storage.

What to Keep in Your Playbook

In your Playbook, keep the last three years of returns, but just the 1040's and the schedules. Don't keep any of the supporting documents in the Playbook; that would get too messy.

You are only going to want to keep the three years of returns so you can: 1) have easy access to the returns in the event you need to apply for a loan or aid and 2) so that your advisors can have access to them in your playbook so they can give you better advice.

Why three years? For most of your potential audit situations, three years applies. However, you can be required to save up to seven years of returns and supporting documents for some circumstances, so often advisors will tell you to save seven years. However, for the sake of advisors giving you advice and for loan or aid applications three years is sufficient.

Long Term Items for Storage

In your long-term storage, you might consider keeping all of your returns. But, you only need to keep the supporting documents for seven years. You might have a system, that once a year at tax-filing time, you go back and eliminates all of the supporting documents for the seven years back as you add a new tax year. The rationale for this? After seven years, the IRS will no longer require you to keep supporting documents, but it could be beneficial to have a copy of the return itself.

Supporting documents are things like receipts, credit card statements, 1099's, W2's. Much of the same information that comes to you throughout the year and that you save to prepare your tax returns.

What Not to Store

The risk of storing anything short-term or long-term certainly isn't that you might need it someday. That's the benefit. The risk is that you are storing it for no reason at all. You can almost create an argument for storing anything, and that's the problem. I might say, don't store that receipt from the drugstore, and you might say, my kids need to know that I once bought aspirin from this drugstore at this time because of a potential future outbreak related to the particular brand of aspirin I used that was manufactured during this particular month. My point here is that we could make an argument for storing anything.

At some point, we have to draw the line in the sand and make a stance against storing stuff. I think of the prudent person rule. Act as any ordinary prudent person would do. Would a prudent person store supporting documents for 20 years when it is not required by the IRS? No, I don't think so. So, I don't think you should do it either. Would a prudent person store notifications from the IRS once the matter has been resolved? Well, maybe, but probably not more than seven years.

Keep in mind that just because you have a long-term storage area for some of your tax related items, that does not give you a good reason to store everything because you don't know what to do with it and because you think a reason might exist in some parallel universe to have this item. You can always come up with some excuse or reason why you need to store stuff.

How the Tax Section of the Playbook Ties into the Rest of the Book

- **The Goals and Objectives section** of your Playbook probably contains some notion of building, preserving, or passing on wealth. Tax efficient strategies are potentially a big part of accomplishing those goals. In the Tax section of your Playbook, you'll see on your returns how efficient your investments are in supporting those goals. Can you look at your tax returns and see if you are paying too much taxes by excess amounts 1099's? Are you maximizing your retirement accounts as indicated by your 5498's? If you have stated values of supporting missions or charities, how does your tax return reflect that? The tax return can act as a scorecard for those goals.

- **The Financial Statements section** of your Playbook contains the Net Worth Statement. This acts as a list of my assets and liabilities. Before I have my taxes prepared, I've got a comprehensive list of all the 1099's, property tax statements, and other documents that I'll need. I can run through my NWS and see what I'm going to need before filing that return. I can say the same for the Cash Flow Statement. It tells me what income is coming in that is going to generate a 1099 or W2 as well as expenses that are going to generate a tax form.

- **The Estate and Legal documents section** of your Playbook has an obvious connection with the Tax section; your final return. Most people will end by having that final return prepared by a professional; self preparation not being an option at that point. Additionally, you might find the need to prepare tax returns for a Trust you have set up at some point.

- **The Insurance section** of your Playbook might contain policies that have some tax deductibility. For example, the insurance on vehicles used for business.

- **The Social Security and Pension section** of your Playbook might lead to some insight about how Social Security is taxed and strategies on how to reduce taxes on your Social Security.

- **The Performance section** of your Playbook is impacted by taxes. It's not always about what you make for a return, sometimes it is what you keep after taxes.

A Playbook Pioneer that comes to mind had a tremendous amount of health care costs that were creating great tax deductions. So, she drew all her income from tax deferred investment accounts like IRAs. When she passed away, she had almost completely drained those accounts and passed on her home and other assets that were tax free to heirs. The kids, although sad that mom was gone, were happy they didn't have to pay taxes on any of the inheritance.

CHAPTER SIX

Performance Reporting

I magine chartering a sailboat across the ocean. Your initial research tells you it's going to take seven days for the trip, so you pack accordingly and set sail. You believe you are on track and making good progress. The wind seems to be in your favor. Then, at nearly the end of day seven, when you are expecting to peer into your spyglass and see land, you see nothing but water. At that point, you decide to reach out to a mapping service only to discover you've been moving along at the wrong speed and have veered off course.

Checking in along the way to see if you are going to accomplish your goals is a pretty smart thing to do, especially if you don't like big surprises. Imagine the anxiety we would experience if we didn't take time on our journey to make sure we were on track and headed in the right direction. When we take the time to write our goals and objectives, it's a great idea to keep track of them in our Playbook as well as keeping track of our progress in our Playbook. That's what the Performance section of the Playbook is all about; keeping track of our progress.

Many of us have set goals for retirement, passing on wealth, providing education for our kids or grandkids, getting out of debt, or just having enough money to live comfortably for our lives. For most of us, these goals require time and a lot of effort. They are worthy and great goals after all. Unfortunately, many people lose sight of their goals after they establish them. Whether it's not enough effort on our part or just bad information that sets us on the wrong direction, we get off track. Staying on course is a great reason to track performance. Performance can provide feedback to keep us on track.

Sometimes it's about relative performance or how we are performing compared to others. Imagine that you are a runner sprinting as fast as you can down a track. Then imagine as you sprint around a corner, someone passes you as if you stood still! Sometimes, when we don't know what is possible, we are under the illusion we are performing at a high level.

Why Do Performance Reporting?

'Performance reporting' might sound like something competitive, and if that isn't your cup of tea, replace performance reporting in this section with status updates. Whether it's status updates on accomplishing your goals or status updates relative to your peers, it's the same idea as performance reporting. Whatever you call it, you should do it and keep track of it in your Playbook.

We measure performance to get an assessment of our progress. That's a must. How do you know if you are going to be able to retire at a desired date if you are not looking at how far you have come and how far you have to go? How do you know you are going to make it out of debt if you don't check-in and see where you are on your NWS and compare it to where you want to be?

160

If You Pay for Advice, Expect to Be Shown Good Performance

If you are working with an advisor, whether it's a financial advisor, a CPA, an insurance agent, an estate planning attorney or whoever they are, you expect them to be held accountable for their performance. In an ideal world, hiring an advisor of any kind should come with performance measures that an advisor builds into the contract of their employment.

If I tell my financial advisor I'd like to retire in 15 years, and we determine how much I'll need and what I need to do to get there from day one, I'll expect to be on track most of the time. If, after ten years, my financial advisor tells me I'm not going to make it, I'll say, "Why didn't you tell me this nine years ago? With five years left, I don't have much time to change directions. Haven't you been measuring my performance along the way?" The answer to that question does me no good at all. Regardless, I'm still not accomplishing my goal that I've been paying someone to help me achieve for the last ten years.

Enter the Playbook. If your financial advisor gave you reports every year that showed your performance as it related to your goals, how would you feel? The ten year we are not on track conversation wouldn't have been a surprise. But you also could have had this conversation a lot earlier and made the changes needed or adjusted your expectations long ago. Performance is the feedback we need so that we can make those adjustments when necessary.

Why Relative Performance Is Important

Imagine yourself on a ladder and the rung you hang on is a representation of your wealth. Above you and below you, as far as you can see, other people clinging to the same ladder. Imagine that at every rung you move up, you are granted a new opportunity or freedom to do something. If you move down a rung though, you lose an opportunity or freedom. Pretend that each person on the ladder is changing positions periodically as well because relative to their peers they are gaining or losing wealth. Some are moving up and some moving down.

At the same time as people are changing positions on the ladder, the ladder itself is moving up and down. As the ladder moves up everyone on the ladder is rewarded with opportunities and freedoms, and as it moves down, everyone on the ladder has freedoms and opportunities taken away.

What I just described is our economy. As our economy flourishes, most of us benefit as our quality of living improves. During times of prosperity, despite where most of us are on the ladder, most of us benefit from strong economy. Even without climbing the ladder, we are experiencing the ability to have more goods and services as long as we are part of that flourishing economy. When we are experiencing a recession, most of us are experiencing to some degree losses or the inability to have as much goods and services.

We are all part of the same system. What would happen to someone who lived in a thriving economy but chose not to participate in that economy? Imagine the ladder moving up but because you are not participating in the economy, you don't move up with the ladder. You just went down a few rungs while everyone else went up. For

162

example, we see people who, even though they have the long-term horizon and even the risk appetite to accommodate a position in the stock market, don't participate in it for one reason or another. When the market roars like we've seen time after time, these people don't benefit from their stock positions going up, the 401ks increasing in value, or their overall wealth increasing as much as those who have exposure to the market.

If most of the people around you are suddenly wealthier as a result of not necessarily hard work or intellect but just the pure exposure to an asset class but you are not, what just happened? Relative to those people, you have lost money. Your position on the ladder has moved down a few notches, not because of anything you did but because of what everyone else did. They participated in the economy, and you didn't. So, you have moved down the ladder, and they have moved up.

If everyone around you is wealthier, they are not only going to be able to afford things that you cannot, but they will put upward pressure on pricing of those resources, making it harder for you to buy them. This is called getting left behind. 'Keeping up with the Jones' isn't about buying all the stuff they have. It's about not losing your position on the ladder without your consent. If you want to minimize and simplify, by all means, do so. But if you are getting acclimated to a certain level of wealth, your position on the ladder, you need to think about your strategy for staying at that position.

That's why performance measurements relative to others is important. We have to keep our eye on what the averages are doing to know if we are getting left behind. It's not the only measure, but it's an important one.

For example, if we planned on an inflation rate of 3% a year over a 20 year period and we assumed we were going to need $3000 a month to supplement our retirement at that time, we'd need just over $5400 in 20 years to feel like the $3000 we want in today's dollars. If we buried our heads and said we're not going to take any risk as long as we are on track for our own goal, we might be just fine.

On the other hand, what if inflation wasn't 3%, but averaged closer to 6% over 20 years? Meanwhile, we've got our heads down and are finding it easy to earn the required rate of return on our investment in very short-term CD's for some reason. In case you don't know already when inflation is higher, interest rates are often rising to slow the economy, and that means CD's yield more. It turns out that the 6% inflation we actually experienced means that our $3000 a month will need to be a little over $9600 a month after 20 years. All the sudden, we find ourselves accomplishing our goals, but we are left behind relative to others who have grown at a rate beyond what we achieved.

I think it's fair to say you have to keep an eye on the performance of others to gauge how comfortable you are going to be competing with them for the same resources. How we compare our performance is a science that is still evolving.

What the Financial Industry Might Tell You Is Important

An entire industry has emerged over the last several decades on performance reporting. Since the 90's when I studied finance, the tools available to the average person, thanks technological advancements, have become too numerous to count. The bulk of the performance measurements have been comprised of a few different variables; mostly the return of an investment, and the risk of an investment.

The Risk and Return Assumptions

The return of an investment should not be subjective and can typically be measured relatively easily. Return will account for capital gains as well as income known as total return. Global Investment Performance Standards (GIPS) would have the total return figure be expressed net of all fees and expenses. That makes sense. It measures the return for the investor after the cost of doing business.

Risk is a little harder to nail down. There are all sorts of risks. For example, there are interest rate risks, liquidity risks, market risks, bankruptcy risks, reinvestment risk, and on and on. When it comes to performance, most measurements of risk have been based on volatility risk or the risk of price variation often measured by an assets price standard deviation. Put another way, when an asset's price moves up and down a lot, it is considered riskier than when the price of an asset doesn't move up and down a lot.

As an example, a house valued at $200k one year, $100k the next year, and $300k the following year and $200k the fourth year would be considered riskier than a house that was worth $200k every year. That's understandable. But, the way volatility as a measurement of risk works, a house that simply linearly declined in value from $200k to $199k over four years would also be considered less risky than the first example. That's something to consider. Even if the outcome isn't as good, the asset could be considered less risky because of less price variation.

Doing performance measurements of assets is more than just looking at the return. It should also account for the risk of the asset. There are mathematical combinations of returns, risk-free rates, standard deviations (risk) along with some other components that attempt to quantify or express a level of risk such as the Sharpe Ratio, Treynor Measure, Jensen Measure, Sortino Ratio, and Alpha & Beta. Again, some of my favorite financial industry jargon. Not important for you to know what they are just that they exist.

The joy of studying the math equations written by economist and business minded money managers is hard to express in words. The good news for those that don't share my enthusiasm for such a past time is this. These measurements for what amounts to return given a certain level of risk are usually prepared for you and readily available. So, given the same return on two different assets, we can choose the asset with the lowest risk because it will have the highest Sharpe Ratio, Treynor Measure, Jensen,…etc.

Here is a potential problem. for the most part although there have been some efforts to correct this but overall, we have not, all of the return information and risk information is based on historical data.

HISTORICAL DATA!! It's what's already happened, not what is going to happen.

When real estate peaked in 2006 it would have had a really high score for return and risk. It wasn't very volatile. It only went up! If you were looking at performance measures at that point, you may have been tempted to buy more; and this, of course, was the worst time to buy. At the bottom of the real estate market in 2012, the performance measures would have told an entirely different story. It would appear the assets were a horrible investment as the returns have been massively negative, and volatility or risk was higher than ever; this, of course, was the best time to buy.

While most people would recognize that if you don't buy at the top of the market and can buy at the bottom, you should be much better off; let's face it, that is hard to do. But, given that, we should still have a natural guard in place that says, "Hey, if the performance looks too good right now, perhaps it isn't the time to buy." And does modern performance tracking tell us that? Maybe. Does modern financial advice and planning suggest we consider that? I don't know, but I think that question begs for us to ask.

Modern Portfolio Theory

Enter _Modern Portfolio Theory_ – the work of Nobel Prize in Economics recipient Harry Markowitz. I won't embarrass myself by trying to express what he did in his work. It won him a Nobel Prize after all. I will, however, summarize it ever so briefly: If you combine the risk of an asset or historical volatility of price, the return of an asset or historical total return of the asset, and the correlation of each asset to each other, you can come up with an optimal portfolio to be created to accomplish your goals given the level of risk you are willing to assume.

The new term here, correlation, refers to how one asset moves up and down relative to another asset. Guess what? It's also based on historical data. So, you put three variables in a bowl, mix them together, and you get a prediction of what's supposed to happen in the future. You are assuming that what happened in the past is going to repeat itself in terms of returns, risk, and how things relate to each other. Let me give an example that hits home. At the end of the buggy whip era, your optimal portfolio for the future would have contained a whole bunch of buggy whips!

OK, so no one can predict the future even based off of historical evidence. No wonder we read past returns are not indicative of future results, thank you legal. So, the next evolution in financial advice is to add in some variability. Enter Monte Carlo Simulations.

Monte Carlo Simulations

Monte Carlo Simulations are not some high-end gambling casino. Instead, a Monte Carlo Simulation is done on software that attempts to factor in the potential for things not to go as planned. Given that we've become accustomed to measuring risk by standard deviation or price volatility, if we make the natural jump to assume a normal distribution of outcomes, we can then claim that things will fall within one standard deviation from the mean 68% of the time, two standard deviations from the mean 95% of the time and three standard deviations from the mean (the average) 99.73% of the time.

This tells us that 95% of the time that things will not fall into the third standard deviation.

Readily available to any financial professional and probably anyone with the interest of looking for it, is software that illustrates a Monte Carlo Simulations. Typically, Monte Carlo Simulations will run 10,000 different outcomes. Some extreme outcomes create a wide range of results.

There are a few variables needed to generate the simulation for retirement planning:

1. The asset classes in which to invest. Assumptions are already included about risk and return for each asset class and again based on what happened in the past.

2. A current age and an age when withdrawals will start.

3. Starting amount of portfolio.

4. Annual contributions and annual withdrawals.

5. Some assumptions about inflation.

What you end up with is a great looking graph like the one below.

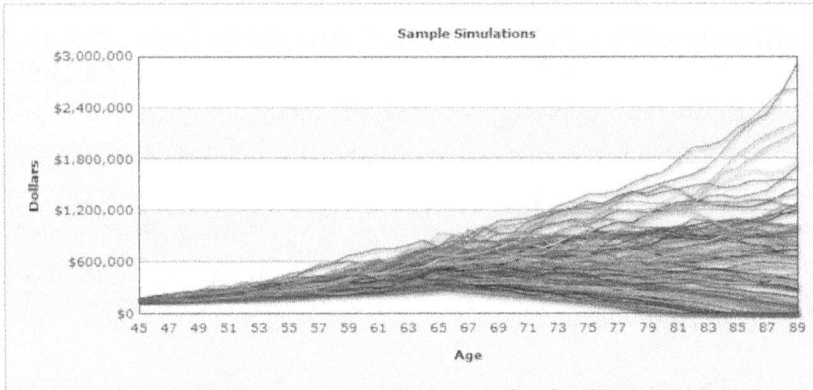

What this graph roughly says is that this 45 year old will, on average, have funds to last through her life expectancy of 89, but the variability of outcomes leaves her either running out of money somewhere around 78 or leaving nearly 3 million dollars as an estate. That is a very wide range of potential outcomes and frankly why in my opinion this type of projection into an unknown future isn't very telling. I don't get much comfort in knowing the potential for all my hard work and planning is going to be so uncertain.

Goal-Based Planning – Perhaps More Relevant

Does a Monte Carlo type simulation really help us? Is it helpful to know that you might die with millions in the bank or run out of money ten years too early? Or would you like to know what the alpha is on your portfolio or how much volatility relative to the market? I suspect that if you are like most people, you care neither for the alpha or knowing what you instinctively know without needing a graph to tell you. The future is uncertain.

So, what do we report when it comes to performance? I've found many people benefit from reporting on how they are accomplishing their goals. We call this goal-based performance. For most people, it seems much more relevant than the previously mentioned approach. Goal-based performance would suggest that you measure the progress towards your goals rather than isolating risk and return numbers.

For example, if you looked into the Goals and Objectives section of your Playbook and you noted that one of your goals was perhaps to create a sustainable income stream during my retirement to guarantee me $5,000 a month in today's dollars after all debt payments by the time I'm 60.

This goal has three parts to track. First, we've got verbiage in today's dollars to consider. Clearly, when you made this goal, you were thinking about how inflation is going to impact your outcome. Because you used the words in today's dollars, I'm thinking you should keep track of inflation over the time from now until you are 60 so we can make sure that your $5000.00 feels like $5000.00. Had you made this goal 20 years ago, for example, you might track this aspect of the goal in the following format where inflation numbers are published each year. By multiplying the previous year's result, you can gauge how much money you are going to need:

Year	Dollar Value	Inflation Rate
1999	$5,000.00	2.21%
2000	$5,168.07	3.36%
2001	$5,315.13	2.85%
2002	$5,399.16	1.58%
2003	$5,522.21	2.28%
2004	$5,669.27	2.66%
2005	$5,861.34	3.39%
2006	$6,050.42	3.23%
2007	$6,222.75	2.85%
2008	$6,461.67	3.84%
2009	$6,438.69	-0.36%
2010	$6,544.30	1.64%
2011	$6,750.87	3.16%
2012	$6,890.58	2.07%
2013	$6,991.51	1.46%
2014	$7,104.92	1.62%
2015	$7,113.36	0.12%
2016	$7,203.09	1.26%

Year	Dollar Value	Inflation Rate
2017	$7,356.54	2.13%
2018	$7,536.22	2.44%
2019	$7,699.82	2.17%*

The advantage of this method is that it blends your actual goal of $5000.00 with the actual performance of inflation. By 2019, you are going to need nearly $7700.00 to feel like $5000.00 in 1999.

The second part of this goal has to do with the guaranteed income. you don't want to risk not having at least this much. For that reason, you might track the guaranteed income amount rather than the dollar amount of your investments. The sources might be from government bonds, CD's, guaranteed investment contracts, fixed annuities, or annuities with guaranteed minimum income benefits. Regardless of the tool you use, tracking the income is the important part.

The third part of this goal is to accomplish the objective by age 60. As we adjust the dollar amount up based on inflation, and we track our progress by adding up all our guaranteed sources of income, we can see how close we are and measure the gap to accomplishing our goals. By keeping track of our progress annually, we can see if we are on pace to accomplish our goal. I've always liked the use of a thermometer chart for a goal like this. It's a nice way to have a good visual of where we are relative to where we want to be.

Another example of a goal might be to eliminate debt when you are retired. This notion seems to be popular again, and I don't think it's a bad idea at all. While it isn't a goal for everyone, I think it's a good goal for many people to have. Here we might track our yearly debt and pick a retirement deadline to have zero debt. I might use something like a graph with a trend line going to zero with points along the x-axis where we can plot our progress.

Regardless of how you track performance, it's important to do. We learn lessons from our success and failures, and tracking performance can help in teaching those lessons. It's also important to note that regardless of how you track performance, it's not important that we all track performance the same way. What is important to you about performance might not be important to others. For example, a runner's success can be measured by either the speed that he or she runs or by the distance.

How the Performance Section of Your Playbook Ties into the Rest of the Book

- Your **Goals and Objectives section** of the Playbook is why we measure performance. The more thoughtful you can be about articulating your goals, the better measurements of performance you are going to develop. It's not some random goal we want to track, it's your goals, and what is important to you.

- **The Financial Statements section** typically embodies much of the household goals. The fruition of your Goals is going to show up on your Net Worth Statement as well as you Cash Flow Statement. If we meet our financial goals, it's going to show up on the financial statements.

- **The Estate and Legal documents section** might have a lot to do with our stated goals and tracking to make sure those goals are met. If we have a Goal of avoiding probate of our estate, we're going to want to make sure we perform routine checks to verify assets are set up correctly. That could be a performance issue; how often do we get 100% in getting the correct registrations?

- **The Insurance section** of the Playbook is often tied to performance. When we don't rely exclusively on ourselves to eliminate risk, we might purchase the help of insurance coverage. Relying on that insurance can help us accomplish our objectives, and that is positive performance that can be measured.

- **The Tax preparation section** of the Playbook might reflect a goal of minimizing estate taxes. If that is the case, I'd want to know before the estate tax event, when I die, if I'm achieving that goal. That's performance. A flow chart showing estate taxes due under certain conditions might be part of a performance analysis.

- **The Social Security and Pension section** of the Playbook will overlap with the performance section when you have goals of minimum income during retirement. These two contributions to retirement income might be part of the thermometer chart mentioned in this section.

From the Playbook Players

The wrong measure of performance

In 2005 we met Bill, an investor who was a little uncertain what his goals were. He had come into some money by way of an inheritance and fortunately knew enough to not spend through it all but rather invest for his retirement and the future. After some modest remodeling to his home, he came to us for investment advice.

In our initial and subsequent discovery, it was apparent that he did not know exactly what he wanted to do with the funds but he did have an expressed goal of not losing money. He wanted his funds invested but he also wanted to have the liquidity available to him in the event he could buy cheap property or a business interest. In fact, he was pretty sure the real estate market was going to open up to him in the next year or two and he'd probably cash out most of his investments to purchase a property.

Given the potentially need for liquidity in his account and the mandate to not lose money, a very conservative portfolio was the only prudent option at the time for us to consider and suggest.

After a few years of earning very modest returns in a conservative portfolio, Bill became very dissatisfied because the stock market had continued to generate great returns. Bill felt like he was missing the boat and being left behind while everyone else made this easy money. Bill was looking at the performance of the market and not looking at the performance of his account accomplishing his stated objective.

In 2007 Bill, against all reasoning, transferred his assets into growth mutual funds so he could also participate in the easy money the market was offering. History shows us the rest of this story. The market started a serious correction in the middle of 2007 as we entered into what is now known as the financial crisis.

In late 2008, after holding on as long as he could stomach it, Bill sold his funds because he had lost too much money in the correction. He was never able to get that property he wanted and eventually spent the rest of his inheritance on another home remodel. He figured he might as well spend it now on something he could enjoy.

What happened with Bill? Well, he focused on performance of what was important to someone else's goals not his own. His goal was capital preservation and he couldn't stop looking at the performance that he wasn't getting instead of what he was getting. This constant looking at performance of what wasn't even relevant to him eventually lead him to purchase the market at one of the worst times in history. This story is even more devastating as a result of selling at the lows of the market. <u>Bottom line, performance should be measured in context to what is relevant for your goals</u>.

CHAPTER SEVEN

Social Security and Pensions

Most of us don't have pensions, right? Many of us think of pensions as a benefit offered in the good old days when you put your time in at work and were rewarded with a good retirement. You got your wages, and when you retired you still got your wages, or some portion of them, for as long as you lived. Over the last several decades, pensions have become less and less common as employers have switched to offering 401k or similar plans that shift the burden of performance to the employee instead of the employer. But we all know that. Back to the question: most of us don't have pensions, right?

In reality, if you work for XYZ Company for so many years and part of your pay is withheld to fund an income stream at a given retirement date, then most of us *do* have a pension. If XYZ Company = anyone subject to a payroll tax, then we all have a pension. It is called Social Security.

In this section, we will cover:

- Why it is important to track the information in the Playbook.
- What to keep.
- What not to keep.
- Decisions to be made with pensions.
- General Social Security questions.

Why It Is Important to Track the Information in the Playbook

Let's face it, you are going to store your social security information, somewhere, right? Or do you just periodically get your statements, if you still get them in the mail, review, and shred? If you do, stop. It's time for a Playbook. If you already have a storage system for your Social Security Statements, rethink your efforts and let me persuade you that adding them to your Playbook is the optimal spot to keep them.

A Few Benefits of Keeping Your Statements in Your Playbook

First, if you are using any form of retirement, work-optional lifestyle planning, you are going to need to know how much your Social Security Payments would be at different ages. Social Security Benefits for many people are a significant portion of their retirement income. Think about it, if you have 2k a month coming in from Social Security retirement benefits and let's say your spouse does as well, that 4k a month is a pretty good starting point for most people. And for some people, all they need.

Do you have any idea how much money you would need to have saved up to generate 4k a month? If you happen to believe the 4% rule for withdrawals, you would multiply 4k by 12 for an annual figure of 48k and divide by 4%. After doing some number crunching, you come up with a figure of $1,200,000.00. Yes, that's 1.2 Million dollars. In other words, if you lived by the 4% withdrawal rate, you'd need to have 1.2 million dollars to equal the income generated by the Social Security pension. Put yet another way, your combined Social Security Payments are worth 1.2 million dollars!

OK, you are analytical and say, "No way! You have forgotten about inflation, liquidity, life expectancy variations, so on, and so on. You are grossly exaggerating in a pathetic effort to make your point. As an educated, analytical reader, I'm not buying it."

To a certain degree, you are correct. We can't compare apples to apples here. One is a gala apple, and one is a red delicious. They are somewhat different, and I don't want to argue about the small variants. The truth, however, is that for most people who would follow the 4% rule, withdrawals from a 1.2 million dollar portfolio are going to act very similar to the income stream obtained from their Social Security retirement benefits. You are welcome to send me your spreadsheets though if you think otherwise.

The point is that Social Security Retirement benefits can be a significant source of retirement income for many people, and if you consider the cost of replacing that income stream, it certainly should merit your attention, especially if you want to head into your work optional lifestyle with a good understanding of how much you are going to have. You've worked hard all those years to get a paycheck, and now it's time for the play check.

Knowing what you are going to have is certainly one benefit of keeping track of things. Being able to communicate that to your advisors, tax, financial, or legal, is certainly another. Over the years of giving financial advice, it's amazing to me how many people will come to me wanting to know what they are going to have at retirement but still can't be pressed to produce a Social Security Benefits Statement.

Fortunately, www.ssa.gov is always at our fingertips. But, even that isn't full proof. To gain online access, you often must enter the maze of riddles regarding your financial history. Answer too many questions incorrectly, and you may find yourself locked out. Eventually, we figure it out, but having statements is certainly handy.

If You Have an Employer-Sponsored Pension

Before discussing the importance of documenting and saving your pension statements, let's first establish a quick definition of a pension vs. a retirement plan like a 401(k):

A pension is an income stream, much like Social Security retirement benefits, that you can expect to receive when you retire. There are many variations of how the payment streams work, but typically it will give you an amount that is guaranteed to last for your life.

Variations of this basic element among other options include joint life with a spouse for the full amount, joint life with a spouse for a partial amount, inflation-adjusted payments, multiple phases with different payment amounts, period certain, cash refund, and so on. The common theme here is that the employer, or pension program, takes on the risk of the investment pool providing those payments. The employee or beneficiary of the payments does not bear the risk.

On the other hand, retirement plans like 401(k)'s work differently. The numbers '401' and letter 'k' don't tell us much other than the section of the Internal Revenue Code that permits the plan to exist. There are many versions of various letters and numbers thrown together, but for the most part, they do the same thing. They establish a type of retirement plan that your employer offers or that you have and the outcome of these investments is what you will eventually have. Examples of these retirement plans are a 401(k), 403(b), 401(a), 457, SEP's, SARPEPS, SIMPLES, and the list goes on and on. The common theme in these types of plans is that the risk of the investments falls to the participants or employees, not the sponsoring entity or employer.

Pension plans, as described above, promise to pay a stream of income at retirement. The funds are controlled by the pension plan itself. The standard of publishing individualized statements once every three years is a minimum and it has been my experience that pensions will publish statements once a year. Regardless, these statements typically are not something you get monthly or even quarterly. You typically cannot access real-time information when you want to about your pension. It's different than a 401k or an IRA where you can log in and get real time values every day. So, when we get statements from pensions, we often file them haphazardly or get rid of them altogether. Retirement is something you'll deal with down the road, right?

On the other extreme, you might be storing more than you need right now because you haven't been able to differentiate between what should and should not be kept. Let's take a look at what is important to hang onto.

What to Keep

Having the right information available to you and your advisors is crucial. In your Playbook, you will certainly want to keep the following:

(1) <u>Social Security Statements:</u> If you don't get one in the mail, most people don't anymore, you will want to visit <u>www.ssa.gov</u> and download your most recent statement.

You will, as previously mentioned, have to sort through a few questions regarding your past to verify you are in fact who you claim to be. But, it's not that complicated, and if you get fouled up you can always call for assistance.

Your Social Security Benefit statement will not only show how much money you can expect to receive in the form of a retirement pension but also a few other important tidbits of information.

For example:

- If you have enough quarters of work fulfilled to qualify for benefits.
- How much your family would receive if you died.
- How much you would receive if you were disabled.
- How much your spouse would receive at retirement based on your earnings.
- If your earnings record is accurate and what to do if it's not.

(2) <u>Pension Statements:</u> If you are one of those lucky individuals who has an actual pension coming to you, you are going to save your pension statements here. But, remember, you only want to save the information in your playbook that would be useful to you and your advisors and is specific to you.

For example, if you have a statement that shows how much money you are going to get, at a certain age, save it. If you have a statement describing the various options for taking income, for example joint with spouse, survivor options, etc.—save it. Your statement might indicate how much money you could potentially get at various ages. Save it, save it, save it. Anything related to you specifically—save it.

These statements are not only a record, and one that doesn't get produced that often, but they will include crucial figures for determining how your future is going to look and how you can make decisions today to make that future look better.

(3) <u>Keep a copy of your Summary Plan Description:</u> this is typically a 12 to 20 page document and contains all the important facts regarding the pension.

What Not to Keep

As always, we run the risk of saving too much stuff. Remember, the purpose of the Playbook is to focus on what is important and to eliminate what is not important. Here, if we saved everything we had related to either Social Security or Pension information, just like with the other sections of the Playbook, we would have a book in of itself. If you are like most people who follow my advice, the Social Security and Pension section of your Playbook will be lean and clean. However, what *not* to keep will ultimately come down to your personal judgment.

Don't Keep the Following in Your Playbook

1. <u>Articles or publications describing social security strategies:</u> Read them and move on. By the time you file, the laws could have changed, and the loopholes may have closed. But there will be others to explore.

2. <u>Pension Reports & Plan Status:</u> These are often reports that tell us how healthy the pension is or how likely it is to meet its obligation; paying the participants. If you are concerned about the pensions financial status, storing the information you get in your Playbook isn't going to do you any good.

Take action. Talk to your HR person or union and figure out a strategy if you have concerns here. Storing notifications only takes up valuable real estate.

3. Paystubs: Yes, they might show how much you put into Social Security and Medicare, but your W2s will include a summary of this information. Look at your Paystub, check it for accuracy, then shred it.

4. Pension management or fund changes notifications: These are merely telling you about a management shift in the fund, something entirely outside of your control. We don't care that the XYZ mutual fund has replaced the ABC mutual fund. If it bothers you, call your HR rep or Union rep.

You don't have to become an expert on what to store and what not to store. What a relief! You have help available to sort through the documents you have. Contact either a plan participant that you know has it already figured out or a representative of your pension plan. Or, if you want professional judgment, hire or visit a specialist in that arena. If you are working with professionals in the financial planning field, talk to them first. It's their job, and they want to help.

General Social Security Questions

The information in this section will not provide a comprehensive guide to all things Social Security; such an undertaking would involve a series of books. And, everyone has a unique situation with different variables that would guide one person in a particular direction and another in a different direction. What we will tackle in this section is some basic Social Security advice.

The good news is, you probably don't need comprehensive Social Security advice that would span a book. If you fall into the category that most people find themselves in, you might survive and thrive with some basic information. But first, a fun fact about Social Security Retirement.

The First Social Security Retirement Income Recipient

Social Security was enacted in 1935 under President Roosevelt. It was created to make sure that retired workers could survive when they no longer could work.

On January 31, 1940, **Ida May Fuller** of Ludlow, Vermont, became the first Social Security recipient when she received a check for $22.54. Miss Fuller, a legal secretary, retired in November 1939. She started collecting benefits in January 1940 at age 65 and lived to be 100 years old, dying in 1975.

Ida May Fuller worked for three years under the Social Security program. The accumulated taxes on her salary during those three years was a total of $24.75. Her initial monthly check was $22.54. During her lifetime, she collected a total of $22,888.92 in Social Security benefits. For her, Social Security really paid off!

The Current Status of Social Security

Recently, the Social Security reserve fund stood at approximately 2.9 Trillion at the end of 2018, according to the annual reports by the trustees. This amount is how much they have in savings to pay future benefits along with gatherings from payroll taxes. The trustees have projected that the cost of the benefits from the Social Security system will exceed its income in 2020 for the first time since 1982. At that point, the balance will start to decline. They estimated, if no changes are made, in 2037 the reserve fund will be out of money. At that point, the ongoing payroll taxes will only be able to pay approximately 75% of the benefits currently promised. This information is clearly published on the social security webpage.

This projection shouldn't alarm or surprise you too much. It has been discussed and debated and as a hard fact of life for decades. Even our Social Security statements indicate right on them that the system will run out of money.

Will Social Security Be around for Me?

One of the most common questions I hear from all walks of life is, "Will Social Security even be around when I collect it?" That is a great question and probably the most important to answer. If Social Security isn't going to be there, why include it in the Playbook at all?

As discussed, the Social Security system is projected to start to run a deficit in 2020. Until now, we have been adding to the reserves. Starting in 2020, we will be eating into the reserves, but we will still have those reserves, and they will last us until 2037. Even at that point though, payroll taxes are still projected to be able to cover 75% or so of the promised benefit. A better question might be, "How much of my Social Security will be available to collect"?

The Social Security system has been changed before and I'll suggest it will change in the future. There seems to be solutions to fix the problem, just a lack of agreement to get the job done. The Social Security Board of Trustees project that changes equivalent to an immediate reduction in benefits of about 13 percent, or an immediate increase in the combined payroll tax rate from 12.4 percent to 14.4 percent, or some combination of these changes, would be sufficient to allow full payment of the scheduled benefits for the next 75 years.

I'd suggest that we plan on some changes. A prudent person might start modeling a 25% reduction as a reality for 15 years down the road. I don't know that a reduction like that would be the worst case, but based on current projections it's at least a possibility.

We can hope though, that the problem is addressed, and our polarized parties come together with a solution. Some combination of raising taxes and curbing benefits is what I would suspect would happen, but I can't see clearly what's going to happen here. Another consideration is that the Social Security Administration under current law is not allowed to borrow money to pay benefits. Probably a good thing as I suspect that's why we have the reserve we do today. But perhaps that will change in the future.

As I write this, (it's April 4th 2020) we're challenged by COVID 19 and that will undoubtedly have an impact on Social Security along with so many other areas of our lives. How our elderly population, our seniors, our loved ones are ultimately impacted by COVID 19 is yet to be revealed but when we get back to business as usual, it will be different business and things will have changed. Let's all pray the world comes together to mitigate the losses from this challenge.

What Happens When One Spouse Dies?

If you are currently collecting Social Security Retirement benefits and one spouse passes away, the remaining or surviving spouse gets to continue to collect the higher of the two benefits. The lower of the two benefits goes away. Let's say Jack and Diane are both collecting, and Jack gets $2000 a month. Diane gets $1500 a month. If Jack passes away, Diane now gets $2000 instead of the $1500 she used to get.

If you are not collecting Social Security benefits and have been married for at least two years, then the surviving spouse will be eligible to collect the higher of the two benefits at retirement. Let's say Jack was 59 when he passed away with a projected benefit of $2000 a month at age 66. Diane, the surviving spouse, would forgo her $1500 a month at retirement and collect Jack's $2000 a month. However, Diane might want to consider the consequences of remarrying. That could impede her ability to collect her deceased spouse's benefits.

What Happens If You Get Divorced?

If you had been married for ten years or more, you could still collect your spousal benefits. Spousal benefits could be either half of your ex-spouses' benefits instead of your own, or 100% of your ex-spouse's if they pass away before you do. However, if you get remarried, you will not be able to file for ex-spouse benefits. But if your current spouse passed away you could elect to receive the higher of the surviving spouse benefit or the ex-spouse benefit.

What If My Ex-Spouse Doesn't Want Me to Collect His/Her Benefit?

Regardless of what your ex-spouse does with his or her own filing, it cannot reduce or deny your claim. They can be as vindictive as they choose, but at least your ex-spouse benefits are secure. And, you don't have to discuss or get permission from your ex-spouse. In some cases it might be better that you don't.

If you are that ex-spouse who is providing the benefit, know that your benefit will not be reduced or altered by your ex-spouse making a claim.

Can I Put More Money into the System and Increase My Payout?

To answer this question, you should know how the payments are calculated. The Social Security Administration uses the top 35 years of earnings to determine your benefit. There is also an adjustment made for each year that brings the dollar amount up to an inflation-adjusted amount. For example, in 1958, $4200 would be multiplied by 13.7 to create a dollar amount of $57,540. If you wanted to replace that 1958 year earning amount as one of your 35 years' worth of income, you would have to make more than $57,540 this year to make it count.

If you have the option of increasing or decreasing your salary due to some additional work you might pick up or if you happen to run your own business with the ability to run more payroll for yourself, then you might consider visiting the detailed calculator on the Social Security Administration Website: www.ssa.gov/planners/calculators/

The more you pay into the Social Security system, the more you will get for your projected benefit. That's pretty clear. The question might be, should you add more to the system? Is it a good payoff? Given the option to add more into the system by paying more payroll taxes now, are you going to get your money back with enough return to justify it?

This question doesn't come up that often, but it's an important one to understand because it gets right at the heart of the issue:

Is Social Security a Good Deal?

If you are self-employed you shoulder the burden of the employer cost as well as the employee cost of payroll. If you are not self-employed you only pay half the cost Social Security and are clearly going to get a better deal. You put less into the system personally but still get the same benefits as a self-employed worker. But, you also might be restricted on how much flexibility you have to control your compensation structure for the sake of manipulating your Social Security benefits. Still, the question of is it a good deal needs to consider not just your cost, but the total cost.

Using www.ssa.gov/planners/calculators/ you can run scenarios of how much Social Security retirement benefits you would get by paying yourself different amounts. The rate of return on each dollar invested in payroll taxes is the question. In other words, for every dollar you put into the system, what type of return are going to get on that dollar? It's clear that the more you pay into the system, up to a point, the more you'll get out of it.

But, what is the rate of return? When I did the math based on my assumptions, I came up with .8%. Point 8 percent, just shy of a 1% rate of return! That means that every time I pay into the Social Security system via payroll taxes, my money is earning me less than 1%. Over the 35 years that I am potentially using for calculating my benefit, I think I can do better than .8% on my own.

There are various assumptions to be made, and as a result, calculations will yield various answers. However, one thing all the calculations tend to have in common is that the rate of return on investing in payroll taxes to increase your social security benefits is very low. I've seen calculations as low as .58%. You might find some higher numbers of 3-4% or even higher, but I'd suggest that those returns don't take into account all the variables for a fair analysis. I think most informed people, particularly those in finance, would agree that the return on Social Security isn't much at all. As a result, anytime the question, "Should I put more into Social Security to maximize my benefits in the future?" comes up, I suggest considering the rate of return first. You might be better off doing something else.

When Should You Collect Social Security?

If you have ever heard that Social Security grows at 8% a year while you are not collecting it, I hope you immediately considered that while your payments would be 8% higher, you've forgone a year's worth of payments.

Traditionally, an approach to determining when to file would be a matter of breakeven analysis. By forgoing earlier payments, you are getting a larger amount of income later.

Take the following example:

*Jack could retire at 62 and collect $1919,

*or retire at FRA *(full retirement age)* of 67 and collect $2741,

*or finally, he could postpone collecting benefits until age 70 and get $3453.

The extra $822 a month by waiting until 67 to collect could come in handy, but you also lost five years of $1919 a month by not starting at age 62. The traditional break-even would say how long does it take to gain that five years worth of $1919 a month back?

In this case, five years, what you lost by not collecting from age 62 until age 67, or 60 months times $1919 = $115,140. Divide that amount by the extra $822 you are getting each month, and you come up with $115,140/822) just over 140 months. That's 11.67 years. So, 67 plus 11.67 years means you have a break-even of 78.67 years. You could draw the initial conclusion that if you live longer than 78.67 years old you would be better off collecting at age 67. And, if you died before that age, you would have been better off collecting at age 62.

You can run the same calculation for 62 vs. 70. In this scenario, you have eight years' worth of $1919 a month to make up for by waiting. That's almost $185k you didn't get that you are going to have to make up with the extra income you get by waiting. (96*1919= 184,224). The extra amount at age 70 is $1534 (3453 – 1919). Divide 184,224 by 1534, and you get just over 120 months. So, at age 70, your break-even point comes ten years later at 80 years of age. Again, we can draw the same initial conclusion. If you live longer than 80 you are better off waiting to collect until age 70. If you die before 80 you are better off collecting at age 62.

Of course, you can run a break-even between 67 and 70 as well. First the difference of 712 (3453 – 2741) and three years' worth of payments of 98,676. We divide the 98,676 by 712 and get 138.58 or 11.55 years. So, your break-even for delaying retirement from 67 to 70 is 81.55 years.

Summary of Break-Even Analysis:

From 62 to age 67. Breakeven – age 78.67

From 62 to age 70. Breakeven – age 80

From 67 to age 70. Breakeven – age 81.55

So, the traditional approach would say that if you live to be 80 or older, plus or minus a year or so, you would be better off waiting to start your Social Security Retirement Benefits until 70. And if you live more than 82 years you are coming out ahead!

I would suggest that this approach fails to recognize the fact that a dollar today is worth more than a dollar down the road. By getting the funds sooner, you have what we call opportunity cost. *Opportunity cost (OC)* <u>has</u> to be factored in, and the above example assumes there is no opportunity cost.

To demonstrate the concept of OC, we can assume that instead of spending the income stream you are getting from Social Security, you are investing it. Let's assume that you collected the income at 62 and never spent any of it. Instead, you invested it in CDs that, on average, paid you 3%. That 3% is your OC. When you earn 3%, you ultimately get more than the $115,140 over the five years from 62 to 67; it's closer to $124,000. If you can invest and get 6%, you would have accumulated nearly $134,000 with your Social Security.

Many of you might say this is ridiculous. Who in the world would possibly save all the Social Security retirement benefits they received? Well, you might be surprised, but whether you save it or not isn't the issue. It's the fact that you recognize OC. Let's say that you didn't invest it in the bank, but instead, you went back to school at 62 for five years. Not that uncommon these days, our seniors often have great aspirations! Check out www.boomerbestu.com.

How do you put a price on that education? What if you didn't have that education by the time you got to 67? Further, once you had that education, let's say you paid $115k for it over five years. What value would that add to the rest of your life? Would it snowball a better life with more prosperity and happiness moving forward? I would hope so, otherwise it wasn't a good investment.

Since it is hard to quantify the rate of return one would get on spending the money now as opposed to in the future, the concept of opportunity cost is a very nice proxy. Finding your own opportunity cost is a personal matter. If you are a CD investor, it might be the 5-year average CD rate you look want. If you are more of a risk-taker, you might push for 5–10%. Once we have an OC to use, we can re-run the break-even on now vs. later.

The table below illustrates the breakeven analysis once we have run the OC of 6%. The income columns are what the retiree would get by collecting at various ages. The balance column is what those accumulated benefits would grow to by earning the opportunity cost. To find the break-even, we simply need to determine when the balances of waiting make up for taking benefits earlier.

I've used 6% only because I firmly believe that over a long enough period of time, a decade or more, you realistically should be able to earn at least 6% And it illustrates my point nicely. When we use 6% as an opportunity cost, we have a new break-even of around 93 years old!

This is a quick analysis that could be open to some criticism. As an example, I compounded annually at the end of each year. There are no considerations for COLAs, and this is, of course, single life projections. More on that later. The point here isn't to get down to the exact dollar amount but rather a pretty good ballpark figure. You could fine-tune the projection, but the break-even would not move significantly.

We had a break-even around 80 years old when you didn't have opportunity cost considered, and now it's out to potentially 93 years old. That's a big difference, wouldn't you agree? And, the higher the opportunity cost, the farther out the break-even is.

Opportunity Cost		6%					
	62 Income	Balance	67 Income	Balance	70 Income	Balance	
62	23028	$23,028.00				
63	23028	$47,437.68				
64	23028	$73,311.94				
65	23028	$100,738.66				
66	23028	$129,810.98				
67	23028	$160,627.64	32892	$32,892.00		
68	23028	$193,293.29	32892	$67,757.52		
69	23028	$227,918.89	32892	$104,714.97		
70	23028	$264,622.02	32892	$143,889.87	41436	$41,436.00
71	23028	$303,527.35	32892	$185,415.26	41436	$85,358.16
72	23028	$344,766.99	32892	$229,432.18	41436	$131,915.65

73	23028	$388,481.01	32892	$276,090.11	41436	$181,266.59
74	23028	$434,817.87	32892	$325,547.51	41436	$233,578.58
75	23028	$483,934.94	32892	$377,972.37	41436	$289,029.30
76	23028	$535,999.03	32892	$433,542.71	41436	$347,807.06
77	23028	$591,186.98	32892	$492,447.27	41436	$410,111.48
78	23028	$649,686.20	32892	$554,886.11	41436	$476,154.17
79	23028	$711,695.37	32892	$621,071.27	41436	$546,159.42
80	23028	$777,425.09	32892	$691,227.55	41436	$620,364.98
81	23028	$847,098.59	32892	$765,593.20	41436	$699,022.88
82	23028	$920,952.51	32892	$844,420.79	41436	$782,400.26
83	23028	$999,237.66	32892	$927,978.04	41436	$870,780.27
84	23028	$1,082,219.92	32892	$1,016,548.72	41436	$964,463.09
85	23028	$1,170,181.12	32892	$1,110,433.65	41436	$1,063,766.87
86	23028	$1,263,419.98	32892	$1,209,951.67	41436	$1,169,028.89
87	23028	$1,362,253.18	32892	$1,315,440.77	41436	$1,280,606.62
88	23028	$1,467,016.37	32892	$1,427,259.21	41436	$1,398,879.02
89	23028	$1,578,065.35	32892	$1,545,786.76	41436	$1,524,247.76
90	23028	$1,695,777.28	32892	$1,671,425.97	41436	$1,657,138.62
91	23028	$1,820,551.91	32892	$1,804,603.53	41436	$1,798,002.94
92	23028	$1,952,813.03	32892	$1,945,771.74	41436	$1,947,319.12
93	**23028**	**$2,093,009.81**	**32892**	**$2,095,410.04**	**41436**	**$2,105,594.26**

94	23028	$2,241,618.40	32892	$2,254,026.65	41436	$2,273,365.92
95	23028	$2,399,143.50	32892	$2,422,160.25	41436	$2,451,203.87
96	23028	$2,566,120.11	32892	$2,600,381.86	41436	$2,639,712.11
97	23028	$2,743,115.32	32892	$2,789,296.77	41436	$2,839,530.83

If I change the variable of opportunity cost, I get the following break evens:

Opportunity Cost	Breakeven from 62 to 67	Breakeven from 62 to 70
3%	Age 82	Age 82
4%	Age 84	Age 85
5%	Age 88	Age 87
6%	Age 93	Age 93
7%	Age 108	Age 103

If you value money more today than you do in the future and if you can put money to work today to create more value for the future, you should assign a reasonable OC to your Social Security Retirement benefits. Once you do that, you will find that the break-even gets pushed out in some cases much beyond our life expectancy.

We need to address some of the circumstances that exist that make the break-even analysis vulnerable. But, before we do that, let's take a look at how your benefits are discounted for early retirement, or increased for deferred retirement.

The following table illustrates, based on the birth year, how much your benefit will be before and after your full retirement age (FRA). Notice that if you were born in 1924, your benefits would be capped at 115% of your FRA amount, and only reduced to 80%. Now compare that with those born on or after 1960. The benefits can be reduced down to 70% and increased to 124%. You can see the shift has been to encourage participants to delay collecting benefits. The break-even analysis we just looked at was for an amount based on 1960 and later. Had we run the break-even analysis for someone born in 1924 it would have been much later even without the consideration of opportunity cost.

Benefit, as a percentage of Primary Insurance Amount (PIA), payable at ages 62-67 and age 70									
Year of birth	Normal Retirement Age (NRA)	Credit for each year of delayed retirement after NRA (percent)	Benefit, as a percentage of PIA, beginning at age–						
			62	63	64	65	66	67	70
1924	65	3	80	86 ⅔	93 ⅓	100	103	106	115
1925-26	65	3 ½	80	86 ⅔	93 ⅓	100	103 ½	107	117 ½
1927-28	65	4	80	86 ⅔	93 ⅓	100	104	108	120
1929-30	65	4 ½	80	86 ⅔	93 ⅓	100	104 ½	109	122 ½
1931-32	65	5	80	86 ⅔	93 ⅓	100	105	110	125
1933-34	65	5 ½	80	86 ⅔	93 ⅓	100	105 ½	111	127 ½

1935-36	65	6	80	86 ⅔	93 ⅓	100	106	112	130
1937	65	6 ½	80	86 ⅔	93 ⅓	100	106 ½	113	132 ½
1938	65, 2 mo.	6 ½	79 ⅙	85 5⁄9	92 2⁄9	98 8⁄9	105 5⁄12	111 11⁄12	131 5⁄12
1939	65, 4 mo.	7	78 ⅓	84 4⁄9	91 ⅑	97 7⁄9	104 ⅔	111 ⅔	132 ⅔
1940	65, 6 mo.	7	77 ½	83 ⅓	90	96 ⅔	103 ½	110 ½	131 ½
1941	65, 8 mo.	7 ½	76 ⅔	82 2⁄9	88 8⁄9	95 5⁄9	102 ½	110	132 ½
1942	65, 10 mo.	7 ½	75 ⅚	81 ⅑	87 7⁄9	94 4⁄9	101 ¼	108 ¾	131 ¼
1943-54	66	8	75	80	86 ⅔	93 ⅓	100	108	132
1955	66, 2 mo.	8	74 ⅙	79 ⅙	85 5⁄9	92 2⁄9	98 8⁄9	106 ⅔	130 ⅔
1956	66, 4 mo.	8	73 ⅓	78 ⅓	84 4⁄9	91 ⅑	97 7⁄9	105 ⅓	129 ⅓
1957	66, 6 mo.	8	72 ½	77 ½	83 ⅓	90	96 ⅔	104	128
1958	66, 8 mo.	8	71 ⅔	76 ⅔	82 2⁄9	88 8⁄9	95 5⁄9	102 ⅔	126 ⅔
1959	66, 10 mo.	8	70 ⅚	75 ⅚	81 ⅑	87 7⁄9	94 4⁄9	101 ⅓	125 ⅓
1960 and later	67	8	70	75	80	86 ⅔	93 ⅓	100	124
Note: Persons born on January 1 of any year should refer to the previous year of birth.									

A Few Problems with the Break-Even Analysis

1. ***It doesn't include COLA's (cost of living adjustments).*** This variable complicates the model and would require a more involved

spreadsheet. However, it doesn't make that much of a difference. COLA's are typically from 2-3% but have been as low as 0 and as high as 14.3% since 1975. Yet they are, unless we get into a very high-interest rate environment, where inflation increases drastically, not that impactful. If we do find ourselves in a high-interest rate high inflation environment, guess what else increases? Opportunity Cost. Remember when CD's were paying 12% or more?

2. *It doesn't account for the dual life expectancy nature of Social Security Retirement Benefits.* Consider that our dual life expectancy is greater than our single life expectancy. If you find yourself in one of the following situations, you should certainly give the choice of when to collect more consideration:

    a. Married and one of you has a much longer or shorter life expectancy than the other. You might consider deferring one benefit to age 70 for the surviving spouse.

    b. Married and one of you has a much higher benefit than the other spouse. You might consider deferring one benefit to age 70 for the surviving spouse.

c. You are divorced, but your ex-spouse, who lives independently, needs to maximize benefits. This isn't just about two lives; it's about two households.

d. Social Security will be your only or majority of your retirement income. Working longer goes hand in hand with deferring benefits.

'File and Suspend' and Other Fun Loopholes

While the rate of return on Social Security retirement benefits might not be that much, the contractual nature of the system itself lends to potential paths that can be advantageous to the participants. Sometimes these are called loopholes, but they are just elements of the system, and understanding how they work can be profitable. Let's take a look at a few of these oddities.

The File and Suspend strategy: This has been readdressed since the Bipartisan Act of 2015. The original strategy, referred to as an "unintended loophole" on ssa.gov, allowed married individuals to start receiving spousal benefits at full retirement age while letting their own retirement benefit grow by delaying it. Imagine Diane, collecting half of Jack's benefit at age 66 while letting her benefit continue to defer at 8% per year. Then at age 70, she switches over to the higher amount.

The change made recently caused the 'file and suspend' loophole to disappear. If you were born after 1954, it's not available for you. If you were born before 1954 you would have taken advantage of it by now. Thus, the file and suspend strategy is a strategy of the past.

The unlimited divorced spouse's loophole, made famous by using the Tonight Show host Johnny Carson as an example, isn't one that people would likely plan to exploit, but still is a fun story. Although this story is possibly true and often presented as true, I don't know that it is. I do know that under the rules set up for Social Security benefits, it is most definitely possible.

An ex-spouse can generally claim half of the Social Security benefit at retirement, and when the primary claimant dies (Johnny), the ex-spouse can claim the full amount. In this situation, here are the rules:

- The marriage must have lasted for ten years
- To collect on an ex-spouse, you can't have remarried
- Your divorce must be at least two years, or your ex must already be claiming benefits
- Both you and your ex must be at least 62

In Johnny's case, he had two ex-spouses who were able to collect half of his Social Security benefit while he was alive. His final spouse potentially collected half of his benefit while he was alive. When he died, both of his ex-spouses, as well as his final spouse, were able to collect his full amount.

Let's see how that would look with a hypothetical amount:

	During Life	At Johnny's passing
Johnny	2000	0
Ex-spouse 1	1000	2000
Ex-spouse 2	1000	2000
Final spouse	1000	2000
Total	$5000/month	$6000/month

So, Johnny and his ex-spouses were certainly able to set up the ultimate quadruple dip! Johnny also reportedly had a third ex-spouse as well but she was only married to him for nine years and thus didn't meet the 10-year mark to qualify for ex-spouse benefits.

Pensions Decisions

Pensions, again if you are lucky enough to have one, are like Social Security retirement benefits in a few ways:

- Similar in that they both offer income for life for the participant as well as typically some options on when to start collecting those benefits. Because of that 'income for life,' we tend to lump pensions in with Social Security in terms of planning and keeping track of important information in our Playbook.

- Typically, once the participant and if applicable the spouse dies, there is no remaining amount to go to heirs or the estate. It's lifetime income only.

- Typically, and most certainly with Social Security benefits, other than potential COLA's, the amount you get is fixed and won't change. They are not subject to market risk in that sense. These figures are thus easy to budget with.

- Both Social Security benefits and pensions have some guarantees in place.

Unlike Social Security, pensions have a few unique features that are certainly worth noting:

- Pension plans can vary considerably. While Social Security is standardized across its benefits and participants, pensions are drafted and customized by the employers offering them. Put another way, a pension at XYZ company can have substantially different options and benefits than a pension at ABC company.

- Pensions, unlike Social Security, typically force the decisions to be made at the time of election with no provision to payback the system and start over. This certainly makes the decision weightier upfront.

- Any consideration for spousal benefits is, again an upfront decision. If you elect single life only, then when the participant dies there is nothing for the spouse. With Social

Security benefits the spousal benefits are built-in and automatic.

- While Social Security is backed by the Social Security Trust fund and in some regard, the credibility of the United States, a pension does guarantee the payments, but it's the pension plan itself guaranteeing the payments. In the words of Tommy Boy, "We both know a guarantee is only as good as the person who writes it." That being said, some pensions are backed by the Pension Benefit Guarantee Corporation (PBGC). We'll discuss that more in detail later.

- Finally, with all of the differences, the ability to request a Lump Sum amount that often exists with a pension contrasts with Social Security benefits where no such option currently exists. Lump-sum gives the participant the ability to cash out of the pension all at once by getting one big check as opposed to getting smaller checks for his or her life.

How Good Is That Guarantee of the Pension?

Who exactly guarantees the pension? You might be surprised that it isn't the company alone sponsoring the pension. That is perhaps a good thing because we see companies go broke all the time; Enron, Worldcom, Sears, and on and on. It's actually the pension plan itself that guarantees the payments. And what is that pension plan? Well, it is just a large portfolio of money. That pool of money is invested in various things like bonds, real estate, stocks, sometimes precious metals, foreign securities, option contracts, and a host of other investments.

A group of companies or individuals run pensions. These are the managers that choose the investments, the actuaries that plan for the incoming payments, called contributions, and outgoing payments called retirement benefits. Typically a board of directors also oversee the pension. These key players, along with support staff are ultimately in charge of the success or failure of a pension. One note, they are not only held to high standards, but they take their job very seriously, and they don't usually take unnecessary risks. That's not an endorsement for any pension fund manager, but rather a statement to say that they often are the cream of the crop in terms of portfolio management.

If those key players are doing well, and the investments are doing well, the pension has a surplus. This is the ideal situation. If the investments are not doing well, the pool of money has a deficit. That's not so good.

You can also have a surplus or deficit when some of the actuarial assumptions are off. For example, if life expectancy is longer than expected, more payments will be made, and that's bad for the pension. If a boon of new employees come on board and funding is high; good for the pension. We won't get into all the details, and there are many more that impact a pension, but it's important to note that the success or failure of a pension really does come down to the investment pool, the assumptions of contributions, and withdrawals. Sounds just like your own retirement, right?

A private sector pension is a stand-alone entity. It has only the assets that it manages to back the promise of payments. If the funds or assumptions don't do well, there is a problem, and the pension managers have some tough decisions to make—the kind of decisions that may challenge a retiree's life. Beyond the pension funds, there is no reputation to worry about, no additional source of tax revenue, and no assets outside of the pension funds. It is a stand-alone entity except an association with the Pension Benefit Guarantee Corporation (PBGC).

The Pension Benefit Guarantee Corporation

The PBGC is a federally created agency established in 1974 by the ERISA act to help make sure that pensions can perform on the guarantee they offer. Wow, that's a relief! The PBGC carefully monitors the performance of a covered pension and collects a premium, kind of like insurance, to help pay for a potential failure of a pension. Typically, a covered pension will pay an amount into the PBGC each year just in case it runs out of money before its obligation or promise is fulfilled. If you have a pension plan, you probably are covered by the PBGC. You can ask your pension contact for a copy of the Summary Plan Description to verify this. Or, you could find this information in your Playbook because you stored it there. Well done!

If your pension plan is covered by the PBGC, what's the risk? It's a federal government-sponsored agency after all. Yes, but there are a few considerations. First, the PBGC has an annual maximum they will protect. If you are looking for a joint pension, one that last as long as you and your spouse should live, retirement at age 65 will come with PBGC insurance up to just over $5,000 a month. Not bad, $60k a year is a good start.

However, if you are forced into early retirement, for example a pilot who is forced to retire at 60, you only get insurance up to just shy of $3,300 a month. And, if you are that hard-working long-time employee who started at age 25 with the hope of early retirement at age 55, you need to know that a joint pension only gets you $2,271.22. All of this is as of 2019. If you are only getting a single life guarantee, the rates are slightly higher; $5,607.95, $3,645.17, and $2,523.58, respectively.

The caps could certainly put a damper on a family's retirement plan, especially if you were are a high earner with expectations of a high pension.

Additionally, the PBGC benefits don't include any COLAs. If you start your pension and are relying on your guarantee from the PBGC, it won't adjust for inflation, and you don't have the potential benefit of participating in a pension surplus if one would occur.

You can find more information on the PBGC website www.pbgc.gov.

The agency protects pension plan participants from the complete devastation of their pensions and adds a great amount of assurance behind private pensions. However, depending on what your pension is promising, the PBGC might not be able to ensure that promise is met to the fullest extent.

United Airlines and the PBGC is probably one of the more notable examples of this in the last few decades. It might be worth mentioning that without the PBGC, it's likely that either the pensions would have defaulted entirely, or United Airlines would have ceased to exist attempting to make up for the pension deficit they had.

Neither of those things occurred, but many participants did take drastic cuts to their promised amounts.

Lifetime Income by Myself, with My Spouse, with a COLA, or a Lump Sum?

The other primary difference between Social Security benefits and a private pension that we can tackle is the difference in the number of choices a participant has in electing his or her benefit. As discussed, pensions can differ drastically. An option that might exist for one plan won't necessarily be available in another plan. For the sake of this conversation, we will focus on some of the more standard options. However, if you have that pension in your retirement pocket, be sure to consult your summary plan description in your Playbook.

How Do I Elect to Take My Pension?

All good pension plans should give you the pros and cons of each option. Lifetime income for you and or your spouse with COLAs is a great option if you want to make sure that neither you nor your spouse outlive your income and keep up with inflation. Consult your Goals and Objectives section of your Playbook. If you want to provide liquidity for your estate and or preservation of the principal assuming you don't need the income, you might consider the lump sum option. There is no correct election when it comes to pension decisions that apply to everyone. The trick is to identify the one that works best for you.

Let's go through some of the common options and identify what attributes might make sense given your particular circumstances:

- <u>Lump-Sum withdrawal to preserve principal:</u> If your goals are to preserve the principal for your estate, this is the option you will probably like the best. It's the option that allows you the most flexibility with your pension asset. You very likely would want to roll it over to an IRA, an Individual Retirement Account that you can have managed on your behalf or manage yourself, account to preserve the tax benefits. If you don't roll it into an IRA, you are likely going to have a mandatory 20% federal tax withheld from the distribution, and the entire amount will likely count as ordinary taxable income. You might find yourself in the highest tax bracket in a given year. Roll it to an IRA, and you don't have the withholding issue or, potentially, the immediate taxation of the distribution.

- <u>Lump-sum withdrawal to get a better return:</u> Careful with this one, right? Know what you have before you walk away from it. In Oregon, where I live, the Public Employee Retirement System (PERS) has been under criticism for years for promising way above average retirement benefits. But still, the option to lump-sum out existed. This isn't an endorsement one way or the other, but many people who 'rolled' out or "lump-summed out" of PERS have had a huge challenge trying to compete with an offer that was, well pretty darn good. The bottom line: Know what you have.

Try comparing your single - life only payment you get from your pension with an SPIA (Single Premium Immediate Annuity). Also, explore guaranteed income stream investments. For example, you might have an income of $5500 a month from a pension, but a guaranteed income stream might offer $5000 a month. On the surface level, you might take the pension. However, you might find the guaranteed income stream allows for the principal to be tapped into, death benefits for heirs, or a continuation of the income to the spouse where the pension might not.

- Single Life, no COLA: This option exists for the individual who wants the maximum amount of income now and isn't overly concerned about inflation or wanting to leave assets to heirs. The COLA, cost of living adjustment, indicates that the payment will increase each year and that increase is usually tied to inflation. The bachelorette or bachelor comes to mind for this selection. The best comparison of whether or not this is a good deal is that SPIA rate you can get from your financial or insurance professional. A Single Life no COLA option is the same as a Single Premium Immediate Annuity. Look at your lump sum value and calculate the SPIA amount you would get with that lump sum. The SPIA should be less than the pension amount; after all it doesn't have the stand-alone risk that a Pension might have. Said another way, a SPIA would be considered safer by most people.

- Single Life with COLA: If you have a long-life expectancy, this one is for you. You will want to keep up with inflation. You will get less per month than you would with no COLA, but it might be worth it to get a raise each year on your payment so you don't feel left behind when things get more

214

expensive. Just be sure to dive into the details and figure out how that COLA is calculated each year.

- Joint Life with or without COLA: COLA now becomes a topic we won't discuss as we just covered it. But the Joint Life concept is new. This option is for the couple that wants to make sure your spouse is covered with the same amount once the primary person has passed. Remember that typically the Social Security benefits will be stepped up to the higher amount for the survivor but the overall impact is that the Social Security benefit will be less because we lose one of the benefits. Keep in mind though that there is one less mouth to feed.

- Joint Life with Partial Remainder: This option can vary a great deal. It might reduce the benefit to 75%, or 50%, or 25%. The trade-off is higher income upfront while both are alive but a reduced amount for the surviving spouse. So many variations exist here like the death of the first spouse could trigger the reduction or the death of only the pension participant could trigger the reduction. Take a look at the details before making a decision.

- Life with Period Certain: For the person that wants the most income possible but doesn't want to run the risk of having the income stream go away if they got hit by a bus on day two. Period Certain means the income would continue to the beneficiaries for the balance of the period. That period could be 5, 10, 15 years or longer. Assuming a Life with 10-year period certain, the pension recipient dies after three years then the payment would continue to her/his heirs for seven more years. I particularly like this option if a household might not need income after a certain period. Say, for example, a mortgage gets paid off in 10 years. Life with 10, sounds like a prison sentence but isn't, would be an option to consider.

There are, as mentioned, so many variables and combinations that exist, it would be hard to cover them all. However, we've covered most of what you will see. I recall the last time I looked at our PERS options in Oregon for taking income, there were 14 different options. Which one to choose is entirely up to the participant, but the decision is a big one. Please consult your Goals and Objectives in the Playbook.

Tying Social Security and Pension Issues into the Playbook

- **Goals, Objectives, and Projections:** If you can't articulate your goals and objectives, you are going to have a really hard time making decisions when it comes to electing how to choose various pension options as well as when to file for Social Security Retirement Benefits. Understanding what is important to you in terms of capital preservation or maximum income is going to impact your decision.

- **Financial Statements:** This ties in particularly strong with the NWS. Knowing what is on your NWS, other sources of liquidity and other assets you have are going to be meaningful in determining how much liquidity you are going to need, and that impacts your Pension decisions. Your CFS is going to remind you of other sources of income you have or will have coming in. That's going to assist you with determining the need for and timing of cash flow.

- **Estate Planning and Legal Documents:** If you elect to get a lump-sum, that's most likely going to impact your estate value, and that might impact your estate plan. Estate planning is a moving target, but income for life versus an actual asset is always going to be an important consideration. Remember guaranteed income for life goes away when you do. So, estate planning might not be a consideration. An asset like an IRA rollover, hopefully stays around after you are not. Time for Estate planning.

- **Insurance Review:** Do you take that life-only pension because it's the highest amount? Maybe, if you have life insurance already in place it is a consideration. Let's check the Playbook for that.

- **Tax Reporting:** Can you imagine the smile on your tax advisor's face if you offered her or him the chance to let you know the tax implications of a straight life pension versus required minimum distributions from an IRA. Not to mention the advanced planning they can do with Lump Sum conversions to ROTH IRA accounts given the right circumstances that create tax-free wealth.

- **Performance Reporting:** If you have the Pension managed for you by the pension fund, you probably want to keep track of how they are doing. Perhaps you notice a rising plan deficit. It might be time to consider other options. Perhaps you see a surplus. Start lobbying for extra distributions. If you manage it yourself, you or whoever you put in charge of that job needs to be diligent and held accountable.

From the Playbook Players

An early retirement that went south

This is a story about a client who was locked into a pension plan that had been very badly mismanaged. The plan assets greatly underperformed their requirements, and as a result the pension modified its projected payouts drastically. The client, who kept hanging on one more year, after year after year, is currently frustrated and still working because his pension amount is no where near where it was originally expected to be, and the PBGC can only do so much. That's the Lathe and Plaster Union Pension.

As you can imagine, they suffered from new employees who would add to the plan in terms of contributions but poor performance as well. Bad performance + bad assumptions = bad outcome.

The Three-Time Winner

Having one pension is pretty cool these days. Having two is *really* cool. Having three is like winning the lottery. Well, this happens. People do actually win the lottery. It's just few and far between.

I'm going to share with you the story of what couldn't have happened to a nicer couple. Both were teachers and had a great pension with PERS (Oregon's Public Employee Retirement System). That's a double whammy right there. Also, one of them retired early from teaching and began a career as an insurance agent. His agency, a large, very well know company, offered a pension plan. Three-time winner! In addition to being lucky with pensions, this couple has also been long-time investors and savers living within their means. We joke now about income problem they have. They have too much of it!

CHAPTER EIGHT

100 Miscellaneous Considerations

Sometimes items clearly belong in one of the other sections. However, having this section is just one more tool in the book to help you keep track of things related to your household.

Here is a list of things that might end up in your Miscellaneous section. While they might fit into one of the other sections as well, they could justifiably put here.

Important Documents to Keep:

1. Honorable Discharge papers

2. Credit reports (run them once a year and keep them here)

3. Username and password list of active accounts

4. List of medications

5. Funeral receipts and instructions

6. POLST – Physicians order for life-sustaining treatment

7. Birth certificates

8. Marriage certificates

9. Citizenship papers

10. Divorce/separation papers

11. Copies of passports

12. Copies of driver's license

13. Allergies

14. Immunization records

15. Copies of certifications or degrees

16. Professional designations

17. Professional organization memberships

18. Faith organization memberships

19. Social club memberships

20. Sports club memberships

Unique Instructions for Your Funeral

21. Who you'd like to speak on your behalf

22. Something you'd like to be remembered by

23. Prepaid funder receipts

24. Burial vs. cremation

25. If cremated, what are your wishes for your remains?

26. Open casket vs. closed

27. Where you'd like to be buried or interred.

28. Instructions on what to bury you with (ring, suit)

29. Obituary ideas/draft

30. Songs to play

31. What you want to wear at your funeral or cremation

Unique Information for Afterward

32. Safe-deposit box location and instructions

33. Hidden Safe location

34. Photo album location

35. Heirloom locations

36. Wishes for urns you may have in your home

37. Pet burial wishes

38. Treasure map for back yard

39. Storage unit information

40. Specific instructions on liquidating a collectible

Regarding Technology

41. Technology access (phone, tablet, computer)

42. Social media wishes

43. Location of digital photos

44. Digital subscriptions in place

45. Security camera information

46. Wi-Fi Instructions

47. Sprinkler system instructions

48. Smart home devices

49. Virtual assistant removal

Subscriptions to End

50. Yard service

51. Streaming services

52. Magazines or publications

53. Cable

54. Satellite Radio

55. Hello Fresh

56. Costco

57. Gym membership

58. Sports ticket renewal

59. Credit card services

60. Water delivery

Words to Your Loved Ones

61. Hidden gems – just in case they forget (a riddle)

62. Personal testimony of faith, philosophy, belief, or vision

63. Letters to loved ones

64. Explanation to your Schedule A (why Jack got favorite knife)

65. Complaint letters (not for everyone!)

66. Where to find a video recording of last wishes

67. Explanation of past life decisions (why you did what you did)

68. What you want to be known for

69. Your favorite sayings

70. The advice you've always wanted to give

If You Are Leaving behind Children

71. Doctor contact Information

72. Their favorite food

73. Their daily routine

74. Any allergies

75. Important health records

76. Favorite hobbies

77. Music preferences

78. TV shows they like

79. Restrictions on what they can and can't watch

80. What is a favorite comfort item for your children?

If You Are Leaving behind a Pet

81. Veterinarian contact information

82. Favorite pet food

83. Favorite treat

84. Daily routines

85. Allergies

86. Favorite toy

87. Best pet friend

88. Social activities

89. Exercise preferences

90. Aspirations (my dog wants to be king of the neighborhood)

Miscellaneous (Even the Miscellaneous Needs a Miscellaneous)

91. Document favorite stories about family (family lore)

92. Items about family culture like crest or symbols

93. Family heritage information

94. Genetic information (ancestry.com)

95. Birthrights (native American rights, royalty connections)

96. Verbiage for tombstone or urn

97. List of favorite books/authors

98. Favorite Games

99. Genetic predispositions

100. Mac or PC preference

Conclusion

Well if you've made it this far congratulations and thank you kind reader! At times in this book I dove deep into details and at others I skimmed the surface. I hope that you found value in the information in the way it was presented and you know that a great deal more information is available on all the subjects from vast resources including the professionals you might be working with.

I also hope that this work has inspired you to organize and address each of the 7 fundamentals of finance. By doing so, I believe you will be empowered to make better decisions and create a framework for effectively managing your household wealth moving forward. By doing so, I suspect you will not only improve your own well being but also ease the burden on those that take over the responsibility for you when the time comes.

So now is the time to take action! Don't hesitate. Get started with organizing right away and remember it all starts with writing down your goals and objectives. Understanding and articulating what you want is challenging but I think it leads to great results.

You might have questions along the way or want further information on the Playbook. Please visit our website where we have a growing number of videos discussing each of the topics covered in this book.

https://elevate615.com/the-playbook-process/ And, feel free to contact me through this site for questions or comments you have. I wish you the very best!

Glossary of Terms

Advanced Directive

Legal documents that allow you to spell out your decisions about end-of-life care ahead of time. They give you a way to tell your wishes to family, friends, and health care professionals and to avoid confusion later on.

https://medlineplus.gov/advancedirectives.html

Annuitization

Annuitization is the process of converting a sum of cash into a series of payments spread over time. Despite the name, most annuities are not annuitized, meaning annuity holders choose not to convert their principal into payments, but rather elect other ways to receive, manage or invest their cash accounts.

https://www.annuity.org/retirement/planning/annuitization/

Asset

An asset is a resource with economic value that an individual, corporation, or country owns or controls with the expectation that it will provide a future benefit.

https://www.investopedia.com/terms/a/asset.asp

Basis

Basis refers to the original price of an asset. It is sometimes called cost basis or tax basis.

https://www.merriam-webster.com/dictionary/basis

Capital Market Expectations

Expectations concerning the risk and return prospects of asset classes, however broadly or narrowly the investor defines those asset classes. Capital market expectations are an essential input to formulating a strategic asset allocation.

https://www.cfainstitute.org/en/membership/professional-development/refresher-readings/2020/capital-market-expectations-framework-macro-considerations

Cash Flow Statement or Budget Worksheet

A personal budget spreadsheet offers an individual a way to determine the state of his finances and help him or her plan spending over the course of a period of usually a month or a year.

https://corporatefinanceinstitute.com/resources/templates/excel-modeling/personal-budget-spreadsheet/

Cost of Living Adjustment (COLA)

The cost of living adjustment is an increase in income that keeps up with the cost of living. It's often applied to wages, salaries, and benefits.

https://www.thebalance.com/what-is-the-cost-of-living-adjustment-3305736

Contingent Beneficiary

A *contingent beneficiary* is a person or entity (such as a charity) that you designate to receive an asset upon your death if the primary beneficiary has died before you.

https://www.legalzoom.com/articles/what-is-a-contingent-beneficiary

Defined Benefit

Defined benefit plans provide a fixed, pre-established benefit for employees at retirement.

https://www.irs.gov/retirement-plans/choosing-a-retirement-plan-defined-benefit-plan

Defined Contribution

Defined Contribution Plan is a retirement plan in which the employee and/or the employer contribute to the employee's individual account under the plan. The amount in the account at distribution includes the contributions and investment gains or losses, minus any investment and administrative fees.

https://www.irs.gov/retirement-plans/plan-participant-employee/definitions

Durable Power of Attorney

A Durable Power of Attorney allows you to assign someone (an agent) to manage your finances if you become incapable or otherwise unable to do it yourself.

https://www.rocketlawyer.com/form/durable-power-of-attorney.rl#/

Health Care Power of Attorney

The *health care power of attorney* is a document in which you designate someone to be your representative, or agent, in the event you are unable to make or communicate decisions about all aspects of your health care. In the most basic form, a health care power of attorney merely says, "I want this person to make decisions about my health care if I am unable to do so."

https://www.legalzoom.com/knowledge/living-will/topic/health-care-power-of-attorney

Home Equity Line of Credit (HELOC)

A home equity line of credit, also known as a HELOC, is a line of credit secured by your home that gives you a revolving credit line to use for large expenses or to consolidate higher-interest rate debt on other loans such as credit cards.

https://www.bankofamerica.com/mortgage/learn/what-is-a-home-equity-line-of-credit/

GLOSSARY OF TERMS

Intestate

Intestate refers to dying without a legal will. When a person dies in intestacy, determining the distribution of the deceased's assets then becomes the responsibility of a probate court.

https://www.investopedia.com/terms/i/intestate.asp

ERISA

The Employee Retirement Income Security Act of 1974 (ERISA) is a federal law that sets minimum standards for most voluntarily established retirement and health plans in private industry to provide protection for individuals in these plans.

https://www.dol.gov/general/topic/health-plans/erisa

ESOP (Employee Stock Ownership Program)

An employee stock ownership plan (ESOP) is a retirement plan in which the company contributes its stock (or money to buy its stock) to the plan for the benefit of the company's employees.

https://www.sec.gov/fast-answers/answersesopshtm.html

Estate Planning

Estate planning is the preparation of tasks that serve to manage an individual's asset base in the event of their incapacitation or death.

https://www.investopedia.com/terms/e/estateplanning.asp

Family Asset

An asset owned by one or both of the spouses and ordinarily used by a spouse or minor child of either spouse for a family purpose is a family asset. For example, the matrimonial home, furniture, and car.

https://definitions.uslegal.com/f/family-assets/

Form 1040

Form 1040 is used by U.S. taxpayers to file an annual income tax return.

https://www.irs.gov/forms-pubs/about-form-1040

Form 1099

The 1099 form is a series of documents the Internal Revenue Service (IRS) refers to as "information returns." There are a number of different 1099 forms that report the various types of income you may receive throughout the year other than the salary your employer pays you.

https://turbotax.intuit.com/tax-tips/irs-tax-forms/what-is-an-irs-1099-form/L3NxSPMUe

Form 5498

Form 5498 reports your total annual contributions to an IRA account and identifies the type of retirement account you have, such as a traditional IRA, Roth IRA, SEP IRA or SIMPLE IRA. Form 5498 will also report amounts that you roll over or transfer from other types of retirement accounts into this IRA. When you claim a deduction for your IRA contributions, you should reference the amounts on the Form 5498.

https://turbotax.intuit.com/tax-tips/investments-and-taxes/what-is-irs-form-5498/L2P16IOdN

Form K-1

The Schedule K-1 is an Internal Revenue Service (IRS) tax form issued annually for an investment in partnership interests. The purpose of the Schedule K-1 is to report each partner's share of the partnership's earnings, losses, deductions, and credits. It serves a similar purpose for tax reporting as one of the various Forms 1099, which report dividend or interest from securities or income from the sale of securities.

https://www.investopedia.com/ask/answers/09/k-1-tax-form.asp

Form W-2

A W-2 tax form shows the amount of taxes withheld from your paycheck for the year and is used to file your federal and state taxes.

https://turbotax.intuit.com/tax-tips/irs-tax-forms/what-is-a-w-2-form/L6VJbqW15

Global Investment Performance Standards (GIPS)

The GIPS standards provide an ethical framework for calculating and presenting a firm's investment performance history. The definition of the firm is the foundation for firm-wide compliance and creates defined boundaries for determining total firm assets. Only firms that manage actual assets may claim compliance with the GIPS standards. To claim compliance, a firm must comply with all the applicable requirements of the

GIPS standards. Compliance cannot be met on a composite, pooled fund, or portfolio basis and can be met only on a firm-wide basis. For example, if a firm definition includes both equity and fixed income products, the firm cannot present only its equity products (strategies) as being in compliance with the GIPS standards. If a firm definition includes both segregated accounts and pooled funds, the firm must meet the GIPS standards requirements for both segregated accounts and pooled funds in order to claim compliance with the GIPS standards.

https://www.cfainstitute.org/-/media/documents/code/gips/gips-standards-for-firms-explanation-of-provisions-section-1.ashx?la=en&hash=3DDE653F82EBE3537DE24D4AABF09FA2A9484AB0

Liability

A liability is something a person or company owes, usually a sum of money.

https://www.investopedia.com/terms/l/liability.asp

Living Will

Living wills and other advance directives are written, legal instructions regarding your preferences for medical care if you are unable to make decisions for yourself.

https://www.mayoclinic.org/healthy-lifestyle/consumer-health/in-depth/living-wills/art-20046303

Long Term Asset

Noncurrent assets. Assets that are not intended to be turned into cash or be consumed within one year of the balance sheet date. Long-term assets include long-term investments, property, plant, equipment, intangible assets, etc.

https://www.accountingcoach.com/terms/L/long-term-assets

Long Term Liability

A long-term liability is an obligation resulting from a previous event that is *not* due within one year of the date of the balance sheet (or not due within the company's operating cycle if it is longer than one year). Long-term liabilities are also known as *noncurrent liabilities*.

https://www.accountingcoach.com/blog/what-is-a-long-term-liability

Lump-Sum Withdrawal

A lump-sum distribution is the distribution or payment within a single tax year of a plan participant's entire balance from all of the employer's qualified plans of one kind (for example, pension, profit-sharing, or stock bonus plans).

https://www.irs.gov/taxtopics/tc412

Modern Portfolio Theory

Modern portfolio theory (MPT) is a theory on how risk-averse investors can construct portfolios to optimize or maximize expected return based on a given level of market risk, emphasizing that risk is an inherent part of higher reward. According to the theory, it's possible to construct an "efficient frontier" of optimal portfolios offering the maximum possible expected return for a given level of risk. This theory was pioneered by Harry Markowitz in his paper "Portfolio Selection," published in 1952 by the Journal of Finance. He was later awarded a Nobel prize for developing the MPT.

https://www.investopedia.com/terms/m/modernportfoliotheory.asp

Monte Carlo Simulation

Monte Carlo simulation is a technique used to understand the impact of risk and uncertainty in financial, project management, cost, and other forecasting models. A Monte Carlo simulator helps one visualize most or all of the potential outcomes to have a better idea regarding the risk of a decision.

https://towardsdatascience.com/the-house-always-wins-monte-carlo-simulation-eb82787da2a3

Net Worth Statement or Balance Sheet

A net worth statement is simply a personal balance sheet. It shows where you stand financially. It provides a summary of your assets minus your liabilities. In other words, your personal net worth is calculated by listing all that you own, and then subtracting all that you owe to get a net number.

https://financialmentor.com/calculator/net-worth-calculator

GLOSSARY OF TERMS

Opportunity Cost (OC)

Opportunity costs represent the benefits an individual, investor or business *misses out on* when choosing one alternative over another.

https://www.investopedia.com/terms/o/opportunitycost.asp

Payable on Death (POD)

A payable on death account, or POD account for short, is a special type of bank account that is recognized under U.S. state law. POD accounts can be set up for checking accounts, savings accounts, money markets, and certificates of deposit as well as U.S. savings bonds. A POD account allows for the money remaining in the account, when the account owner dies, to pass to directly to the beneficiaries named by the account owner. It will happen outside of probate, and in general, all that the beneficiaries of the POD account will have to do to gain control of the account after the owner dies is to show the bank manager an original death certificate for the owner.

https://www.thebalance.com/what-is-a-payable-on-death-or-pod-account-3505252

Pension

A pension is a retirement fund for an employee paid into by the employer, employee, or both, with the employer usually covering the largest percentage of contributions. When the employee retires, she's paid in an annuity calculated by the terms of the pension. Pension funds are far less common than they used to be, with labor unions and public employees making up the vast majority of pension holders.

https://www.bankrate.com/glossary/p/pension/

Pension Benefit Guarantee Corporation (PBGC)

Congress set up PBGC to insure the defined-benefit pensions of working Americans. Defined-benefit pension plans are traditional pensions that pay a certain amount each month after you retire. If you have a pension from a private-sector job, you are probably one of the 40 million Americans covered by PBGC insurance protection. PBGC insures more than 26,000 pension plans.

https://www.benefits.gov/benefit/1074

Per Capita

Under per capita, the share of any beneficiary that precedes you in death is shared equally among the remaining beneficiaries. Within a beneficiary designation, per capita typically means an equal distribution among your children.

https://www.mastrylaw.com/whats-the-difference-between-per-capita-and-per-stirpes-beneficiary-designations/

Per Stirpes

If a named beneficiary precedes you in death, then the benefits would pass on to that person's children in equal parts. Spouses are generally not part of a per stirpes distribution.

https://www.mastrylaw.com/whats-the-difference-between-per-capita-and-per-stirpes-beneficiary-designations/

POLST

POLST = Portable Medical Orders. POLST forms are medical orders that travel with the patient (your state may call it something other than POLST).

https://polst.org/

Power of Attorney

A power of attorney (POA) is a document that allows you to appoint a person or organization to manage your property, financial, or medical affairs if you become unable to do so.

https://www.legalzoom.com/articles/what-is-a-power-of-attorney

Primary Beneficiary

The primary beneficiary is the person or entity who has the first claim to inherit your assets after your death. Despite the term "primary," you may name more than one such beneficiary and designate how the assets will be divided among them.

https://www.legalzoom.com/articles/contingent-beneficiary-vs-primary-beneficiary

Probate

Probate is the formal legal process that gives recognition to a will and appoints the executor or personal representative who will administer the estate and distribute assets to the intended beneficiaries.

https://www.americanbar.org/groups/real_property_trust_estate/resources/estate_planning/the_probate_process/

ROTH IRA

A Roth IRA is an individual retirement account that offers tax-free growth and tax-free withdrawals in retirement.

https://investor.vanguard.com/ira/roth-ira

Schedule A

Use Schedule A (Form 1040) to figure your itemized deductions. In most cases, your federal income tax will be less if you take the larger of your itemized deductions or your standard deduction.

https://www.irs.gov/forms-pubs/about-schedule-a-form-1040

Sharpe Ratio

The Sharpe ratio was developed by Nobel laureate William F. Sharpe and is used to help investors understand the return of an investment compared to its risk. The ratio is the average return earned in excess of the risk-free rate per unit of volatility or total risk. Volatility is a measure of the price fluctuations of an asset or portfolio.

https://www.investopedia.com/terms/s/sharperatio.asp

Short-Term Asset

A short-term asset is an asset that is to be sold, converted to cash, or liquidated to pay for liabilities within one year.

https://www.accountingtools.com/articles/what-is-a-short-term-asset.html

Short-Term Liability

A short-term liability is a financial obligation that is to be paid within one year.

https://www.accountingtools.com/articles/2017/5/16/short-term-liability

Single Premium Immediate Annuity (SPIA)

A single premium immediate annuity, or SPIA, is a contract in which you pay an insurance company a lump sum, or a premium, in exchange for guaranteed, periodic payments for life or over a set period of time. A SPIA can begin paying out income almost immediately after you purchase it. People purchase SPIAs to fund retirement.

https://www.annuity.org/annuities/immediate/

Springing Power of Attorney

Like a durable power of attorney, a springing power of attorney can allow your attorney-in-fact to act for you if you become incapacitated, but it does not become effective until you *are* incapacitated. If you are using a springing power of attorney, it is very important that the standard for determining incapacity and triggering the power of attorney be clearly laid out in the document itself.

https://www.elderlawanswers.com/powers-of-attorney-come-in-different-flavors-8217

Standard Deviation

In statistics, the **standard deviation** is a measure of the amount of variation or dispersion of a set of values. A low standard deviation indicates that the values tend to be close to the mean (also called the expected value) of the set, while a high standard deviation indicates that the values are spread out over a wider range.

https://en.wikipedia.org/wiki/Standard_deviation

Term Life

Term life insurance provides death protection for a stated time period, or term. Since it can be purchased in large amounts for a relatively small initial premium, it is well suited for short-range goals such as coverage to pay off a loan or providing extra protection during the child-raising years.

https://www.statefarm.com/insurance/life/term-life

Time Value of Money

The time value of money is a basic financial concept that holds that money in the present is worth more than the same sum of money to be received in the future. This is true because money that you have right now can be invested and earn a return, thus creating a larger amount of money in the future.

https://corporatefinanceinstitute.com/resources/knowledge/valuation/time-value-of-money/

Transactor

In the credit card world, a transactor is a cardholder who transacts—that is, makes purchases with a credit card—but does not carry a balance and therefore pays no interest charges. The derisive term in the industry for transactor is "deadbeat." The counterpart of a transactor is a "revolver"—one who uses the card and carries a balance, incurring interest charges.

https://www.creditcards.com/credit-card-news/glossary/term-transactor.php

Transfer on Death (TOD)

The transfer on death designation lets beneficiaries receive assets at the time of the person's death without going through probate.

https://www.investopedia.com/terms/t/transferondeath.asp

Trust

A trust is a legal instrument that allows property to be passed to heirs and beneficiaries without going through probate.

https://www.merriam-webster.com/dictionary/trust

Will

Many people keep their will in file cabinets, safe deposit boxes, offices, or with an attorney. You need the official document to begin the probate process

https://www.everplans.com/articles/what-you-need-to-know-before-you-submit-a-will-to-probate-court

Whole Life

Whole life insurance is a type of permanent life insurance (also called cash value life insurance), which is one of the two categories of life insurance. (The second major category is term life insurance).

The biggest difference between these two categories is that term life insurance ends after a set number of years; it offers a death benefit and nothing more. Permanent policies like whole life, on the other hand, cost more because they include an extra savings component, which is referred to as the "cash value."

https://www.policygenius.com/life-insurance/whole-life-insurance/

Acknowledgments

I'm very proud of the work we've done as a team to create and use the Playbook in our practice. My business partner Daniel Nordstrom, CFP, MDIV, and Kay Lang—veteran stock trader and operations manager extraordinaire, have been instrumental in helping me get the Playbook process dialed in and ultimately launched.

I'm thankful for the financial advisor mentors I've had in my career. Craig Verdi, CFP of Verdi Wealth Planning, helped me to learn how to focus intently to listen to my clients and hear their real concerns, and understand what was actually important! My good friend Linda Paxton demonstrated true empathy for her clients and her work ethic I've yet to see duplicated now decades later. She showed me just how much you can care for the people with whom you do business. Finally, my loving wife who reluctantly turned over the household finances to me early in our marriage. Marki, your patience and understanding as I learned first-hand what it takes to manage the personal household finances was a test of patience. Your support and encouragement for the work I do continues to be a source of fuel and motivation.

I also want to thank each of my clients over the years for what I've learned from you. Collectively, we've covered a lot of ground and I'm thankful for the trust you've placed in us and the opportunity to have served you. Many of you have helped with editing suggestions (B.E., D.Y., C.V. and P.U. extensively). Your input on helping me clarify my message was extremely helpful. And to C.B.; you are the Godmother of the Playbook! Thank you for your inspiration and your determination to organize and address the 7 fundamentals of financial planning. Not only for yourself but for your loved ones.

www.ingramcontent.com/pod-product-compliance
Lightning Source LLC
Chambersburg PA
CBHW022035190326
41520CB00008B/593